The Friend
We Have in Jesus

The
Friend
We Have
in Jesus

Rudolf Schnackenburg

Westminster John Knox Press
Louisville, Kentucky

© 1997 Westminster John Knox Press

Translated by Mark A. Christian from *Freundschaft mit Jesus*,
by Rudolf Schnackenburg,
© Verlag Herder Freiburg im Breisgau 1995

Book design by Jennifer K. Cox
Cover design by Pamela Poll
Cover illustration: Head of Christ, by Rembrandt van Rijn.
Gemäldegalerie, Dahlem-Berlin, Germany. Courtesy SuperStock.

First edition
Published by Westminster John Knox Press
Louisville, Kentucky

This book is printed on acid-free paper that meets the
American National Standards Institute Z39.48 standard. ♾

PRINTED IN THE UNITED STATES OF AMERICA
97 98 99 00 01 02 03 04 05 06 — 10 9 8 7 6 5 4 3 2 1

Library of Congress Cataloging-in-Publication Data

Schnackenburg, Rudolf, 1914–
    [Freundschaft mit Jesus. English]
    The friend we have in Jesus / Rudolf Schnackenburg
        p.   cm.
    Includes bibliographical references.
    ISBN 0-664-25731-3 (alk. paper)
    1. Jesus Christ—Person and offices.   2. Friendship—Religious
aspects—Christianity.   I. Title.
BT202.S354513   1997
232'.8—dc21   97-23138

Contents

Introduction

ho was Jesus of Nazareth and what does he mean for us today? How does he give our lives direction? Toward what goal is he leading us? I have mused over these questions time and again. And from the early days of my scholarship I have asked historical and linguistic questions in accordance with the historical-critical method, which examines the words and deeds of Jesus that have been passed down to us through the centuries. My reconstruction therefore has clearly not been formed by way of an unqualified acceptance of a dogmatic theology, for instance by starting with the assumption that Jesus is the Son of God, the Messiah, and the Savior of humanity from sin and death. Scientific deduction is necessary and leads to an ever-clearer image of Jesus. The current dispute regarding the person and intentions of Jesus is unavoidable for those who think about their faith; through it, ever-new aspects of the person of Jesus Christ are elucidated and brought into the discussion.

When we ask the question, "Who is Jesus for us today?" our approach has everything to do with the results we gather. For instance, if a contemporary approach emphasizes what Jesus Christ means to the individual, it places the subjective (for instance, the effects that Jesus produces in the hearts and souls of humankind) before intellectual considerations. For there are various impressions, or impacts, of the person of Jesus Christ. There is an objective impact, deriving from the history of events and of ideas. This may be said of philosophy, anthropology, and cosmology as well. On the other hand, there is a subjective impact depending on the individual's perception, will, and search for meaning. In the end however, the subjective and the objective must combine for any standardized formulation of Jesus Christ to emerge, one that is organically flexible, adaptive to both rational and emotional claims. Achieving and maintaining this goal necessitates a perpetual balancing act between reason and experience.

In writing this small book in sickness and old age, I have striven to keep the feeling and experiential impact of Jesus Christ clearly in view, concerning myself especially with young people who are laboring to construct their own image of Jesus. I ask myself, How can the figure of Jesus Christ become engaging—even fascinating—for the youth in our midst?

Various encounters and experiences have answered this question for me, firmly implanting the idea that each person must conclude for himself or herself that Jesus is the friend—indeed the personal friend—of every human being.

Friendship is a multileveled sphere of human experience; it is at the same time laden with emotion and rationally constituted. Furthermore, it seems to me that the very persons who speak about such friendship are those who desire it; they then are the ones who are able to find it. This being the case, I am able to envision friendship with Jesus as a light on the horizon within the darkness of our time. It is not easy to grasp this great hope, however. Such a discovery occurs only after removing other influential portraits of Jesus, which Part One of this book should accomplish.

One example of an undiluted, fully actualized portrait is that of the "revolutionary" Jesus. Furthermore, it is important to note that the perception of "the revolutionary" in Jesus has changed significantly during the past decade. Formerly this characteristic was typically interpreted either politically or by emphasizing its bellicose aspects; whereas today we find social and societal aspects being given greater emphasis. Take for instance Jesus' radical moral demands, his cultural critiques—and, if you will, his religious critiques, which is how one may interpret Jesus' attacks on both the religious establishment and the religious leaders of his time. And while times and circumstances have certainly changed, today's society manifests phenomena that would have assuredly evoked an angry response from Jesus. Indeed, just as Jesus challenged a restrictive and obdurate Judaism, so would he also contend with today's crusty church—a church out of touch with modern life, a church that bears his name but has not carried out his intentions.

Given this background, Jesus' reputation as a revolutionary is surely understandable. Further, his longing for something beyond an empirically defined church proves quite attractive for those today who, while considering themselves Christians, are nonetheless critical of the church. Indeed, the portrayal of Jesus as "revolutionary" is wholly compatible with the portrayal of Jesus as friend.

Another characteristic emerges for those who would see Jesus paralleling the Qumran community to the point that he resembles a secret participant within that Jewish sect. Such a fantastic theory as "Jesus among the Essenes" is very problematic, though, and therefore must bear the burden of proof. With or without proof, however, Jesus as the friend of all humanity must be distinguished from Jesus the Essene.

Part One will conclude with our treatment of Gerd Lüdemann's thesis[1] that has recently caused so much excitement: that the crucified Christ did not rise from the dead; on the contrary, his disciples' belief in the resurrection originated in visions. We are not dealing with something essentially new here, but rather an interpretation that, while seeming quite plausible to moderns, has shown itself capable of destroying the comforting nearness of Jesus. These attempts at a rational explanation do not, however, strike at the heart of our relationship with Jesus. Rather, they act merely as a negative foil for the living relationship with him that falls into the category "friendship with Jesus."

Introduction

Following our treatment of these still-flawed interpretations, we will turn in Part Two to the theme of "friendship with Jesus," developing it with the aid of biblical texts. It is my hope that this picture will be a fascinating one. Different aspects of friendship become clear if we attend carefully to the places in the Bible that speak about the friendship of Jesus: in everyday life, with others, at meals and festivals, in times of distress.

Friendship must also prove itself genuine during times of persecution and suffering. This is why Jesus spelled out his disciples' futures to them, their destinies, the sacrifices that were ahead. Martyrdom has proven attractive to Christians throughout the centuries, and Jesus promises martyrs life with him in God. Furthermore, friendship with Christ, even in sickness and frailty, leads to a strength that prevails over bitterness, weariness of life, and all desperation.

The Johannine writings describe a particular school of friendship and brotherly love that we will examine in detail. It transcends the prosaic notion of friendship, expanding it even into the realm of mystic thought. Here we see Jesus in a role much beyond that of human capability, but one that we may nevertheless participate in, drawn into, as it were, his communal fellowship with God.

Friendship with Christ is an inner becoming as well as an existence in Christ. Such a deeper dimension of friendship revitalizes the Holy Spirit within us. It does so as long as we take seriously this relationship which is made available to us. The onus is upon us to decide for or against this relationship. We might add that one cannot grasp the depth and riches of Christian faith without venturing upon this quest. This book will likely inspire only those who would be willing to take such steps.

Part One

PORTRAITS OF JESUS

Chapter 1
Picturing Jesus

ince the inception of Christianity people have been occupied with the following question: Who was Jesus of Nazareth, this man who came forth at the beginning of our era in the small land of Palestine? He attracted a large Jewish following to his cause but kept chafing against the powerful resistance of the district leaders until he, this man so mindful of humanity's plight, fell prey to the persecution of his enemies. Among the clearest things about Jesus are the circumstances surrounding his rebellion against the power of the Roman state, and his dealings before Pontius Pilate, who allowed him to be executed, sentenced to death on a cross. Which portrait of this man, however, do we accept? He proclaimed the kingdom of God, healed many who were sick, and strove to bring the love and compassion of God to humanity. This is the portrait painted by the Gospels, which are practically our only sources on the life and death of Jesus of Nazareth.

The evangelists were convinced that the crucified Christ did not remain dead; rather, God revived him, endowing him with new life, a life that continued through the community of believers, the church. From this time forward Jesus was called "Christ" ("anointed one"). Jesus of Nazareth's names and honorific titles are so distinct, in terms of religious meaning and historical perception, that there is little doubt that these designations evidence an unquestioned pool of common belief from which the evangelists drew: He is the promised Messiah, the Son of God, who has freed humanity from sin, guilt, and death; he has given new life.

This divergence of opinion concerning Jesus' origin, works, and death, not to mention the debate surrounding the evangelists' reliability, is what prompted my book *Jesus in the Gospels: A Biblical Christology*.[1] This book falls into the category of "Quest of the Historical Jesus" research, which, since the Enlightenment in the eighteenth century, has by and large grounded its scientific focus in a preoccupation with the "person" of Christ. This rationale, however, whose scientific method has taken particular note of historical and philological findings, has manifested a conspicuous lack of consensus about working procedures. Further, it has not once led to a convergence of the differing standpoints. This, then, was the impetus behind my decision to distill the viewpoints of the four evangelists in the above-named work. In it I have also included an explication of my more recent views. It is my hope that these efforts will enable new insights into the person of Jesus Christ. It is not necessary to go into this now; I would only suggest that the reader bear in mind that the four evangelists each convey a different picture of Jesus, and that their corporate vision of Jesus Christ somehow, upon closer analysis, results in mutual agreement.

From the outset—as has been mentioned already—the foundational matrix of the Gospels is not free of problems, and we need to deal with these problems head-on. However, our primary task is not merely to sketch Jesus' portrait, so to speak, for this has already been done, perennially and from earliest times. Moreover, these ruminations on the person of Jesus Christ have in no small way been "helped along" in their growth and development, to the point where a definite orientation can be discerned.

As a result, a markedly fideistic reconstruction has emerged, a viewpoint shaped by faith. Add to this the further extrapolation brought about through christological debate, and we are left with something that corresponds very little to the original picture of the historical Jesus. Recognized as the central issue in the "Quest of the Historical Jesus" research, the question was stated thus: How does one determine the relationship between the "historical Jesus" and the "Christ of faith"?

I would prefer not to enter into this endless dispute right here; instead I would simply ask: Which reconstructions of Jesus Christ have stood out in the past and yet retain contemporary significance, generating discussion even to the present? Albert Schweitzer's brilliant late nineteenth- and early twentieth-century interpretation (*The Quest of the Historical Jesus*) yielded reconstructions that were quite different.[2] What is more, he clarified the failure of the Quest of the Historical Jesus, which was based on subjective judgments and preconceived notions. Schweitzer maintained his position to the end: "Jesus does exist in our world, yet as something intangible and indefinable. This reality is neither shaken nor strengthened by historical knowledge, but it is true nonetheless, because a powerful stream has gone out from him, flowing even into our time."[3]

Werner Georg Kümmel has reviewed this discussion,[4] concluding that the literature on Jesus is dismaying and scarcely comprehensible; in short, it seems as though at the present time a state of utter chaos reigns. He is also convinced that a historical-critical preoccupation with the personage of Jesus of Nazareth leads to certain preordained findings.

Numerous characterizations of Jesus have arisen through the years: Jesus the freedom fighter, who wanted to free his people from the alien Roman power but was frustrated by the stark reality of the political circumstances. Jesus the moral philosopher, who promoted strict—even radical—moral demands and strove to bring about a social upheaval, a reordering of society; Jesus the enraptured enthusiast, who perceived the approaching end of the world and sought to prepare humankind for it; Jesus the religiously observant Jew, who fell into sharp conflict with the Pharisees and teachers of the law; an urbane Jesus, whose demeanor squared well with his social stratum; a mythological hero of sorts, whose profile clearly surpassed that of the historical characterization of Jesus of Nazareth, at times actually falsifying it and various other portraitures.

Although a kernel of truth exists in some of these varying portraits, they are not deserving of widespread acceptance, sympathetic reading notwithstanding. In the present work I have opted for a view of Jesus Christ whose analysis does not end with the examination of historical evidence; rather it is an investigation into the "yet-living" Jesus Christ. For example, he is known to exist within the hearts of many awe-filled people, people who are virtually carried away by his moving acts of love: *Jesus my friend, the friend of all humankind*. We are dealing here with the influence of Jesus on those who are engrossed in his person. This is where they wish to understand and build their lives.

Jesus transcended things historical and temporal and spoke to individuals in search of meaning for their lives in a way that in the end found grounding in his being. I can therefore readily accept what Albert Schweitzer perceived as timeless. Jesus Christ has come into the world: "a powerful stream has gone out from him, flowing even into our time."

With such a "stream" in mind, we ask this question: Is it necessary, then, to consider these new provocative discussions coming onto the scene, whose reconstructions of Jesus are targeted primarily at young people? These depictions stand in partial antithesis to the interpretation that would characterize Jesus as friend, as the friend of all humanity. But they also accept and then extend earlier positions, though necessarily "repackaging" them according to contemporary notions regarding the range of human understanding and knowledge.

In view of these attempts to understand Jesus anew, and to construe him according to the "history of ideas," I would like to deal briefly with such interpretations of the person and meaning of Jesus,

6

according to the following headings: (1) the Revolutionary Jesus, (2) Jesus of the Essenes, (3) the Crucified but Not Risen Jesus. After tracing these reconstructions we can then raise our claim, giving it careful and judicious treatment, arguing in favor of the theme "Jesus, my friend" as a paradigm for the younger generation.

Chapter 2
The Revolutionary Jesus

uring the early years of the Quest of the Historical Jesus, the thesis arose that Jesus was a political rebel endeavoring to liberate his people from Roman rule. This thesis doubtless belongs to the strongest and most inveterate strain of Jesus reconstructions considered thus far. Hermann Reimarus (1694–1768), a philosopher and theologian of the Enlightenment, advocated this position.[1] He is considered the founder of the Quest of the Historical Jesus movement. Furthermore, it can be demonstrated that this repeatedly revived thesis has kept things stirred up even up until the present.

We know much of bloody revolution: the horrors of World War II, the brutal Nazi reign of terror wherein millions of Jews were murdered. Those who escaped in 1945 are still, to this day, so traumatized by reenactments of armed conflict that any subsequent attempt at promoting war—for any reason—is now rejected from the outset: "No more war!" "Power to the powerless!" "No more ethnic cleansing!"—so go the watchwords.

Nevertheless we find that in the Jesus literature the allegations of failed uprisings of both Jesus and his disciples are maintained, making themselves heard again and again. Robert Eisler's two-volume work, whose Greek title may be translated "Jesus, the King Who Did Not Reign,"[2] caused quite a stir. The American scholar Joel

Carmichael expanded Eisler's thesis with his *The Death of Jesus*.[3] S.G.F. Brandon, a British scholar, in his book *Jesus and the Zealots*, endeavored to prove that Jesus was somehow connected with the Zealots, a party advocating violent revolt.[4]

The arguments that support these theses have been employed time and time again: the "purification of the Temple," representing Jesus as a powerful man of action, is naturally supported by the young, who see Jesus wanting to seize control of the Temple while at the same time heralding the onset of the revolt against the Romans; a Zealot among the ranks of the disciples (e.g., Simon the Cananaean, or the Zealot; perhaps including Judas Iscariot also); the sword-bearing and sword-wielding associated with Jesus' arrest; some of Jesus' sayings such as Luke 22:36, "And the one who has no sword must sell his cloak and buy one," or Matthew 10:34, "Do not think that I have come to bring peace to the earth; I have not come to bring peace, but a sword." In order to understand these verses (cf. Luke 12:51–53) one must interpret them simply as direct commands. It is maintained that all these traditions date from after 70 C.E., the year of the destruction of Jerusalem accomplished by the Roman emperor Titus, and that these traditions were apologetically and pacifistically effaced by the evangelists.

To be sure, all these arguments have long since been refuted—for instance, by Oscar Cullmann in his book *Jesus and the Revolutionaries*,[5] and by Martin Hengel in *Was Jesus a Revolutionist?*[6] The thesis that Jesus' disciples made a vigorous political stand finds few advocates anymore. Nevertheless, would not Jesus have gathered some revolutionaries about himself during the course of his opposition to the district's Jewish rulers? No one would deny that he sharply criticized the religious praxis of Jerusalem's high priests. Further, this was no doubt the occasion that led to his trial before the high council. The high priests spared no effort making sure Jesus was indicted by the Roman tribunal, whose armed Temple district patrol then seized him. In this way the Roman authorities constructed an accusation of political rebellion against a Temple desecrater, whom they of necessity liquidated.

The Revolutionary Jesus

This is an enlightening theory. It explains how Jesus was sentenced by way of Roman justice.[7] Accordingly, Jesus was no political agitator; rather, the high priests were alone in the allegations they raised before Pilate, the man who in the end allowed his execution as "The King of the Jews." Jesus' cleansing of the Temple was a prophetic, symbolic act. To the Sadducean high priests, however, it was perceived as an attack, and one that afforded them the opportunity of having Jesus dragged before the Roman forum. Be that as it may, Jesus displayed his critical attitude toward the Temple in a way that was clearly neither political nor militaristic but, rather, religious in nature. And even though Jewish observers likely perceived him as "revolutionary," it was the Jewish religious leadership proper—its cultic religion and its strict codes of law-observance—against which Jesus took such a critical stance.

It is certainly no mere accident that the model of the "revolutionary" Jesus was recast recently in the student revolts of 1968. In a similar way we have seen the gospel used to justify guerrilla warfare on behalf of poor, oppressed, and mistreated persons in Latin America. Among the combatants were Christians, working under the direction of their priests. Accordingly, the Colombian priest Camillo Torres stockpiled and dispatched weapons from his church office. He lost his life in a January 1966 skirmish with government troops. For Torres, affirmative action on behalf of the oppressed and suffering of humanity meant armed confrontation.

In sharp contrast, Jesus did not preach violence and murder; rather, like Mahatma Gandhi, he strove for nonviolent liberation. Moreover his motive to save humankind from its misery, again like that of Gandhi's, was religious in nature. Jesus looked to divine intervention for the liberation of the poor levels of society, and through his message he described the coming kingdom of God. As forecast in the Song of Zechariah, Jesus announced a liberation in which God has saved us "from our enemies and from the hand of all who hate us. Thus he has shown the mercy promised to our ancestors, and has remembered his holy covenant, . . . to grant us that we,

11

being rescued from the hands of our enemies, might serve him without fear, in holiness and righteousness before him all our days" (Luke 1:71–75). The tenor here is unmistakably subversive and is consonant with that of Mary's Magnificat: "He has shown strength with his arm. . . . He has brought down the powerful from their thrones, and lifted up the lowly; he has filled the hungry with good things, and sent the rich away empty" (Luke 1:51–53).

Here we encounter a line that can also be construed as "revolutionary": Jesus was no political rebel; rather, a social reformer. He spoke out against the propertied class and the rich and wanted to bring about a new social order, yet not through the use of force; rather though the power of persuasion. He proclaimed, as it were, a revolution of the heart. This issue is attested elsewhere in Jesus' message. From the very beginning he speaks of the blessedness of the poor, of the woes reserved for the rich, of stringent demands: the renunciation of all possessions, and of the need to follow after him in lowliness and poverty. Thus these texts are, to be sure, well known, and yet we repress rather than receive them.[8]

Jesus indeed communicated an "option for the poor" and this he "implanted in the heart," an expression that has been prominent in connection with the liberation theology of Latin America, demonstrating that a strong desire for economic and social reordering reigns in our time also. People want to orient their lives according to Jesus' message. By this I mean that the paradigm of the "revolutionary" Jesus does have contemporary relevance, although on a different level: no power politics but rather a social revolution.

While reviewing the Jesus literature, one can see how the attempt to describe Jesus as a social revolutionary who speaks to the social conditions of recent times has come about, especially through the socialist movement. Some of the pioneers advocating the liberation of the working classes employed just such a portraiture of Jesus. In his book "The Origin of Christianity, a Historical Investigation,"[9] Karl Kautzky met with a positive response from the workers, "the proletariat"; so also did Max Maurenbrecher with his work "From

Nazareth to Golgotha."[10] These works intensified the class struggle of their time. Their conceptual point of departure, while finding its orientation in Jesus, has declined in value of late because of social development and improved working conditions. To be sure, the social problems of the nineteenth century—especially unemployment—remain; and the disparity continues between rulers and ruled, rich and poor, where in each case the latter are still dependent on the former.

It is in this way that the "social revolutionary" Jesus remains a challenge, especially to the church establishment. I am convinced that the voice of Jesus, as it has been understood in the past, still indicts the rich while welcoming the poor. This hermeneutic serves as a background for our theme "Jesus my friend, the friend of all humankind."

Chapter 3
Jesus of the Essenes

n recent years the thesis has been put forward that Jesus showed affinity with the Qumran community, had contact with them, was filled with their thoughts, and strove for the exact same things that the Qumran community wanted. As a result, a completely different picture of Jesus has arisen than the one related to us by the evangelists. Jesus was wholly different, and the early Christian movement must necessarily be viewed in a new light.

This thesis, "Jesus of the Essenes," is not new. K. H. Venturini advocated it in a decisive manner in his work "The Natural History of the Great Prophet of Nazareth" (1800–1802).[1] In 1970 Johannes Lehmann caused a sensation through a broadcast series on the south German radio network and a panel discussion in a church broadcast titled "The Secret of Rabbi J." According to Lehmann, the secret of Rabbi J (= Jesus) is to be explained by the fact that Jesus belonged to the Essenes; moreover, he appropriated their teachings. The author attributes the basis of this thesis to the Qumran writings, the most important of which had largely already been published at that time. His book "Jesus Report: Record of a Falsification"[2] concerned itself with a further expansion of his position. This propagated and provoked responses from the press.[3] At that time I, together with my students Karlheinz Müller and Gerhard Dautzenberg, succeeded in forestalling the spread of an extensive conflagration brought about as a result of these interpretations of Jesus. Nevertheless, here we are twenty years later replaying the same publicity-induced game, though now on a new level and with much greater response.

Michael Baigent and Richard Leigh, both expert journalists, published a large work in the early 1990s that was accompanied by considerable publicity, *The Dead Sea Scrolls Deception*,[4] which almost became a best-seller in Germany. The authors expected their book to overturn all prior knowledge about Jesus and act as an explosive device, while an external cause, namely the publishing of additional Qumran texts (for example, the so-called Temple Scroll from Cave 11, and other more or less important fragments), had an intensifying effect. It is against this background that the sensational thesis of both authors is to be read: that a Vatican plot existed, whereby highly controversial texts brimming over with vital information were suppressed. These texts would supposedly yield a completely different picture of early Christianity. An analysis of the Qumran texts would mean that the history of Jesus and of early Christianity must be entirely rewritten.

The book deals with three thematic areas: (1) new information about the Qumran scrolls; (2) the construction of a plot in the Vatican; (3) a revolutionary reconstruction of Jesus, for whom the apostle Paul in particular is brought in as a witness. With regard to their theses, the authors refer to the American professor Robert H. Eisenman, of California State University, who published *The Dead Sea Scrolls Uncovered*, in which he displayed fifty major documents from the more recent discoveries, translated and interpreted. These texts were expected to demonstrate conclusively the early Christian character of the whole Qumran textual corpus. However, each text remains completely within the mind-set of this particular Jewish group, and there is no single text that allows for Christian interpretation proper.

The conspiracy in the Vatican is an absurd supposition because the Dominican "suspects," scholars in the field of international research from the well-known École Biblique et Archéologique in Jerusalem, were not at all in the position (nor were they at all willing) to suppress certain alleged highly controversial texts.

Furthermore, the reconstruction of the text is outlandish. An important role is played by James, the Lord's brother, whom Baigent and Leigh identify with the "Teacher of Righteousness" and declare to be the leader of the Jewish freedom movement. This James resided in Qumran and was even proclaimed the rival high priest. The Jewish high council tried to subdue the revolt with force. At the same a Jew with the name Saul distinguished himself, soon recognizing that the resistance movement could become strong only if it produced martyrs. As a result of this, Paul is supposed to have feigned his conversion and wormed his way into the inner circle of leadership. With his interpretation of Jesus' mission and sacrificial death he then created a new religion. But the Roman authorities staged a mock fight in order to arrest Paul. Therefore early Christianity was, in actuality, a revolutionary freedom movement, one that the evangelists somehow obscured. This, in rough detail, is the interpretation of the two authors Baigent and Leigh, who illustrate a variant view of Christianity's revolutionary origins.

All these positions have long since been refuted. It is certain that the Qumran texts' provenience is not a Christian one and that all identifications of the figures of early Christianity that coincide with those of Qumran spring from pure fantasy. The whole affair has become somewhat like a mystery novel, as Heidelberg professor Klaus Berger has observed.[5] The mystery plays itself out on two different fronts: (1) within early Christianity, and (2) as a modern plot. The particular questions that we may discuss in detail are: How similar are the Qumran texts in relation to the Gospels? And what similarities exist between the Qumran community and early Christianity?

Joseph A. Fitzmyer, a profound scholar and expert on the period in question, has written the book *Responses to One Hundred One Questions on the Dead Sea Scrolls*.[6] Also Otto Betz, a pioneer in Germany's

Qumran research, together with his student Rainer Riesner, wrote the volume *Jesus, Qumran and the Vatican*,[7] which provides the essential clarifications.

Even more fantastic than *The Dead Sea Scrolls Deception* is the book written by the Australian professor Barbara Thiering, *Jesus from Qumran: His Life Rewritten*.[8] She wants to compile evidence that Jesus stemmed from the Qumran society, and that his life took a completely different course than is described in the New Testament. Especially spectacular is her thesis that Jesus did not die on the cross; rather he drank an analgesic concoction that rendered him unconscious, but the people of Qumran revived him. Jesus married Mary Magdalene, fathering a daughter and two sons. After being revived, he lived approximately thirty years, divorced his wife and married a Greek named Lydia, a dealer in purple cloth in Philippi, who is mentioned in Acts 16:14.

These are all empty claims, without any support in the texts. The mock death of Jesus, not a particularly new "theory," was already ruled out when Jesus' execution was attested by Roman historians. New to the currents of thought that appeal to contemporary fancy are Ms. Thiering's speculations into the alleged love ties of Jesus to Mary Magdalene, their divorce, and the subsequent marriage to Lydia. One wonders how a respectable publisher could impose such a book upon its readers.

And yet the dispute regarding the Essene character of the Jesus movement is making waves even within serious research. Therefore I would like to deal with this matter in more detail. If one concludes that Jesus was not a member of the Qumran community, the question then presents itself as to whether he sympathized with that group and advocated similar views. Based on some of the more recent findings, the position is taken that Qumran texts made their way into the New Testament. So then, when did the Qumran writings arise?

In general we date their genesis to the period from the second or first century B.C.E until Qumran's destruction in the Jewish War of

68 C.E. Thus it is possible that some of the Qumran writings were contemporaneous with those of the evangelists, or that they originated from their preliminary stages. The Spanish papyrologist O'Callaghan wanted to identify 17 fragments with statements in the New Testament, among which was 7Q 5, to be identified with Mark 6:52f. Accordingly, Mark's Gospel would have originated earlier, perhaps in the 40s. However, the identification of such small fragments is still disputed; an interdependence between New Testament texts and those of Qumran has yet to be established.

Yet another thesis that we take serious exception to: Did Jerusalem have an Essene quarter? On the authority of the excavations in southwest Jerusalem, some believe that they have discovered it in the vicinity of the contemporary Dormition Abbey of the Benedictines, near the traditional Upper Room. The Catholic researchers Bargil Pixner, O.S.B., an archaeologist, and Eugen Ruckstuhl, an exegete, have argued vigorously in behalf of this thesis. It is thought possible that Jesus held his last communion in an Essene quarter, and even according to Essene religious praxis. If so, the time, place, and circumstances of the Last Supper would have to be determined otherwise. Indeed, the chronology of Jesus' last week—the trial and passion—would turn out to be different. The upshot of the matter is that the likelihood of an Essene colony in Jerusalem cannot be contested; proving such a reality, however, is another matter.

The New Testament makes certain statements that could be interpreted as referring to the Essenes. Acts 6:7 states that a large number of priests took up the faith. It could refer to Essene priests converted to Christian beliefs. Even that, however, remains uncertain. The Essenes are not mentioned in Rabbinic literature either; no doubt because, subsequent to Qumran's destruction in 68 C.E., they no longer played a significant role in Judaism. In reference to the Essenes being an influential group in the Judaism of the time, it is only through the Jewish history writer Josephus that we come to know them, and through Pliny the Elder, who reported in his *Natural History* that they lived above En-Gedi on the Dead Sea. That can only refer to the Qumran settlement. Finally, the religious philosopher Philo (c. 25 B.C.E. to 40 C.E.) made note of the Essenes in one of his writings, according to which the Essenes separated themselves from the rest of the people and lived an aesthetic, rigorously regulated life.

A symposium took place in Graz, Austria, in 1993 concerned with points of contact and characteristics that the Jesus movement shared with the Qumran Essenes. Walter Kirchschläger, the New Testament scholar from Lucerne, addressed the topic "Qumran and the Early Christians." According to Kirchschläger, what connects the Qumran community with Jesus is, first of all, their shared origins in Judaism. Contemporary Judaism had different streams and groups that were akin in their understanding of Jewish life and the Torah, and in their eschatological expectations, and yet again clearly differed. To such belonged the Pharisees with their strict juridical observance, the antiquated and bound-to-tradition Sadducees, Zealots striving with force for liberation from the Roman yoke, and priestly-minded Israelites, among them the Qumran community with its emphasis on the Zadokite priesthood.

One clear connecting link to the Jesus movement can be seen in the repentance movement brought to life by John the Baptist, even though John the Baptist cannot really be forced into a Qumran community mold. John's contribution, a baptism for the forgiveness of sins in order to avoid God's judgment, differed somehow from the many purification baths that had been practiced in Qumran. Jesus stood near to the preacher of repentance from Jordan, greatly honored him, indeed to the point of being baptized by him. Nevertheless Jesus significantly distanced himself from him through his message about the in-breaking kingdom of God. The ritual baths in Qumran and their holy meals find certain affinities with Christian baptism and with the eucharistic meal; however, upon closer examination they are seen to be different rites.

Accordingly the differences between Qumran, Jesus, and the early church should not be overlooked. Perhaps the most serious is the different view of people who strive toward the salvation of God. According to the Rule of the Community from 1QS 1:9f., the participants should all live as sons of light, but they should hate all sons of darkness, each according to their iniquity. Qumran proclaims the God of justice; Jesus, on the other hand, proclaims the God of love and mercy. He becomes the helper and friend of all humanity.

An important figure in Qumran is the so-called "Teacher of Righteousness," a man originating in the priestly sphere, one who may also be seen as the main founder of the Qumran community. When we compare what we know about the "Teacher of Righteousness" with the life and works of Jesus, one notable difference presents itself: the numerous healings of the sick that transpired through Jesus. In Qumran, the physically challenged were not accepted; what was desired was a pure and holy people. Jesus took upon himself the miseries and the sins of the notorious. "Those who are well have no need of a physician, but those who are sick," he said (Mark 2:17). There are many further differences in the interpreting of laws and in religious praxis. Indeed, one cannot say that everything in Qumran was different, but rather that serious differences do indeed exist between this Jewish group and Christianity, that the two religious movements cannot be equated. If we place Jesus within the network of Jewish religious parties, his uniqueness and otherness become crystal clear. "Jesus of the Essenes" is the product of tightly controlled and misguided historical observation; consequently the Jesus movement it delineates is different from the earliest Christianity depicted in the New Testament. The comparison with the Qumran community can only make clearer our view of "Jesus our friend and the friend of all humankind."

Chapter 4
Jesus: Crucified but Not Raised to New Life

 t is appropriate here for us to turn our attention to yet another interpretation of the person of Jesus Christ, one which from the very beginning of the Enlightenment was further expanded, remaining virulent up into our time and shattering belief time and time again: It is said that one cannot cling to the view that the Jesus who was executed on the cross was raised from the dead and appeared to the disciples. Clearly that is a premature, albeit prevailing, belief that does not stand up under historical and text-based scrutiny.

To be sure, this rationalistic critique finds a hearing again and again, even to the present time, thereby destroying the fundamentals of Christian belief. For the resurrection is in fact the basis of living faith in Jesus Christ, who died but was raised to continue in a new way as the ever-living Lord, the one who could say, "I am with you always, to the end of the age" (Matthew 28:20). The apostle Paul wrote with all clarity to the Corinthians, who did not want to accept the belief in their own resurrection, "If the dead are not raised, then Christ was not raised. And if Christ was not raised, then our preaching is empty and our faith senseless" (1 Corinthians 15:13f.); and in another place, "If the dead are not raised, then Christ was not raised. But if Christ has not been raised, then your faith is useless, and you are still in your sins" (15:16f.); or, "If we have set our hope on Christ only in this life, we are to be pitied above all other humans" (15:19).

The belief in the resurrection has existential meaning for Christians. It impacts their earthly life and gives it direction, content, and meaning. If we give up these beliefs, the bond between us and Jesus is severed; he ceases to be our helper and friend. The resurrection therefore is the cornerstone of our belief and an undeniable component of our creed. However, it is just this article of faith that, from the time of the Enlightenment until today, has been questioned again and again.

Not so long ago a book by Gerd Lüdemann, a Protestant theologian, appeared bearing the title *The Resurrection of Jesus: History, Experience, Theology*.[1] In this work the author sets for himself the goal of investigating anew the whole complex of questions—especially the New Testament witnesses—and comes to the following conclusion: "So Good Friday ended in silence as in a dark cave, and thus the torch lit by Jesus was evidently snuffed out in an ice-cold way. However, not long after the death of their master on the cross and the return of the disciples to Galilee a new spring unexpectedly dawned. We do not know precisely when this happened. . . . But not long after the Friday on which Jesus died, Cephas saw Jesus alive in a vision which also had auditory features, and this event led to an incomparable chain reaction" (174). Upon final analysis, then, the whole Easter belief traces its origin to a vision of Simon Peter that is continued in subsequent visions. "The first vision to Peter proved formally 'infectious,' and was followed by others."[2]

One must acknowledge the exceptional competence with which Lüdemann deals with all the critical questions about the New Testament text, calling into account matters concerning the resurrection of Jesus and the witnesses of that resurrection, in fact scrutinizing the material according to the historical-critical method and with extreme care. We can also understand how he came to the conclusion mentioned above. But the reduction of the Easter faith to visions, however one may explain them, naturally remains shocking to all who believe in Jesus, the crucified and risen One. Moreover, we will also find it necessary to question whether all of the particular analyses that the author undertakes in this book (33–171) are equally valid and convincing—for example, the analysis of the proclamation of the risen One at the empty tomb (109–21). Nevertheless, the historical misgivings merit serious consideration, in which case there appears to be nothing conclusive or historically verifiable left standing. Only faith can cope with the unclear, semi-legendary, and contradictory reports.

The work's conclusion is all the more surprising, where Lüdemann poses the question: Can we still be Christians? In his answer he advocates the view that all historical and theological explanations offered in behalf of the actual resurrection of Jesus are "apologetic digression maneuvers to evade history" (180). Nevertheless the author does not wish to jettison Christian belief, remarking, "To the question 'Can we still be Christians?' the answer has to be a confident 'yes' " (182). In saying that, he is supporting himself on the humanity of Jesus that confronts and challenges us in the Gospels. "The man Jesus is the objective power that is the enduring basis of the experiences of a Christian. . . . Jesus grasps me, makes me bow down, exalts me and makes me blessed, loves me, through all the strata of the tradition. He is the ground of faith" (ibid.). The decision of faith therefore falls upon the historical Jesus—not upon the risen Christ.

This conclusion sounds good, but the question presents itself as to whether we are actually able to encounter the yet-living Christ: "We must stop at the historical Jesus, but we may believe that he is also with us as one who is alive now" (183). But just how are we to arrive at this belief, that he is with us? To be sure, it is possible only if we are convinced, along with the early church, that the historical Jesus through his resurrection and exaltation on high still dwells with us below.

It is an erroneous alternative: to hold on either to the historical Jesus or to the risen Jesus. For the early Christians, the two were inseparably bound together. On the whole, they were convinced that they could attain legitimate access and a true understanding of the efficacious Jesus, who once walked the earth, only through the resurrection of Jesus. This is the reason the disciples, on their descent from the Mount of Transfiguration, were warned that they should tell no one about what they had seen, "until after the Son of Man had risen from the dead" (Mark 9:9). All conversation about what Jesus had done and said first became possible for the disciples only after Jesus fulfilled his destiny. One can only understand it if the crucified "Son of Man" was revived by God.

Indeed, in connection with Lüdemann's theses we ask yet more precisely: Just what are we to make of those visions of Peter and the other witnesses to the resurrection? "Visions" are, to be sure, the most widespread and popular attempt at explaining that which was witnessed or described in the reported "appearances" to the Disciples and the women who went to the tomb (Mary Magdalene!).

It is said that to these persons the risen One was "apparent" (Greek: *ophthe*), an expression that can mean "he was seen," or "he was made visible" (that is, by God), or "he has made himself visible." Today this "becoming visible" is taken to mean a "vision." The text speaks at times (John 20:18, 20; 1 Corinthians 9:1) of the "seeing" of the risen One. And yet what kind of a seeing was it? Was it an actual bodily sighting? Were they psychogenic visions, in which the longed-for or the imagined is accepted with inner certainty as true reality? Were they dreams originating from external causes or reflections that intruded upon the disciples as realistic experiences?

The expression "vision" is much too unclear and polyvalent a term to explain the expression "appearances" of Jesus. It was a special seeing that became an onerous task for the evangelists to describe.[3] With a naïveté untouched by the problematic question of what constitutes "visions," critical theologians have been speaking about "visions" for a long time. David Friedrich Strauss had recourse to this explanation in his two-volume work *The Life of Jesus, Critically Examined* (1835–36).[4] The seeing, encounter, and experience of the

26

risen One here is said to be a mythical account of the continued existence and contemporary presence of Jesus, early Christian notions dressed up as history.

For Rudolf Bultmann, who decisively championed demythologization, the experiences of the disciples described as visions are only "expression[s] for the meaningfulness of the cross." Also, according to Eugen Drewermann's depth-psychological interpretation, these statements, which arise from mental archetypes, are only to be understood symbolically. In each person resides an irrepressible longing for the afterlife of humanity, as indicated by the expectations and promises of the different religions, especially in Egypt. In Christianity this faith produced its own expression in the person of Jesus Christ. The New Testament appearance reports were nothing more than expressions of the yearning of humanity for eternal life, encoded statements about what the person of Jesus has to say to us. Drewermann adheres to belief in an afterlife of humanity and holds to the words of Jesus, but he does not postulate the bodily resurrection of the crucified One. For him that is a legend that nonetheless contains the deeper truth we have within us, that which assures us of our immortality. Thereupon the testimony of the disciples, who wished to see the dead Jesus alive again, becomes invalid and weak, even superfluous, because what they want to attest, the continuing presence of Jesus, is certain in any case.

Gerd Lüdemann engages all the accounts—including those of the empty tomb and of the tomb visitation of the women, the encounter of the disciples from Emmaus with the risen One, the appearance of Jesus before Peter, and all further appearances—in order to strip them of their historical credibility. Remaining from these narratives, then, are only the visions of those who were convinced about the continuing presence of Jesus, beginning with Peter. Lüdemann remarks, however: "Doubtless one or another point of the historical outline of the earliest Christian belief in the resurrection needs to be corrected. The reason for this is not only the relatively meager amount of source material, but also the nature of the event itself" (175).

However, he thinks there is no "gap" in the sequence of events of the early Christian Easter faith, but rather "a beginning of a religious enthusiasm with its own dynamic. The oldest history of early Christianity runs almost logically" (176).

Since this explanation of the appearances of the risen One as visions resounds naturally and plausibly, we must not entertain any illusions with respect to the consequences of these publications. This Jesus, who was crucified but certainly not raised to new life, holds great appeal for our skeptical, pragmatic, and dispassionately minded humanity. Nevertheless, each person who studies the New Testament carefully must reject this explanation, because it does not do justice either to a historical-critical inquiry or to a portrait of Jesus Christ that is in comprehensive agreement with the New Testament itself.

At this point another image of Jesus needs to be proposed that is still valid for our time, one that can explain the constant turning to his person of broad segments of believing people and account for the powerful stream of belief and love that continues today. Accordingly, we want to develop a concept in Part Two that suggests itself both for the historical picture of Jesus Christ and for his subsequent effects in Christendom: Jesus our friend, the friend of all humankind.

Part Two

JESUS OUR FRIEND—
A FASCINATING PORTRAIT

Chapter 5
The Gift of Friendship

riendship is a priceless gift that life has in store for us. It belongs to the happiest and most sought-after experiences of every phase of life. After all, children want to obtain a little boy or girl friend, wishing for playmates with whom they can associate often, discussing and undertaking all plans together. Childhood friendships may often endure a long time; people will reflect on their childhood friendships throughout their lives. Friendship can develop in one's youth; to be sure, it can also change. Now young men turn their attention to young women, and vice versa. Out of that interest develops close relationships, wherein people want to be together often, longing for intimate nearness. The attraction to the opposite sex intensifies and often leads to youthful love. There is scarcely a young person who doesn't want to have a boyfriend or girlfriend. Growing older does loosen or completely break apart some earlier friendships, and yet it might initiate new ones that can last a lifetime.

Friendship, which can vary greatly in form, is the essence of regard and honor. Older persons cling to the friendships that they have lost in life, which support them during times of darkness and loneliness. Friendship is a gift bestowed on humans, the capability and capacity for reciprocity and trust, for the self-disclosure of one person to another, so that one might participate in the other's joys and sorrows, hopes and fears, successes and failures. The experience of friendship is a blessing.

The High Value of Friendship

The Greeks are considered as the classic people of friendship. Friendship is praised in lofty tones by philosophers and poets, by battle companions and round-table chums, by happy drunks and serious conversation partners. In friendship the desire for happiness is fulfilled and each rapturous joy blossoms, itself raising a "spark from Elysium" over the earth. Friends want to have all things in common, to participate in and live life with each another. These aspects recall Greek understandings of friendship again and again.

The Hebrew language has no special expression for "friend"; it speaks about neighbors, differentiating between those within and without one's own group, and about companions. However, the Old Testament does indeed know the subject of human friendship. An outstanding example is the friendship between David and Jonathan, Saul's son, described in 1 Samuel 18ff. King Saul became David's enemy out of jealousy and envy and tracked him down, seeking his very life. But Jonathan valued David: "Then Jonathan made a covenant with David, because he loved him as his own soul" (18:3). He kept David informed of Saul's whereabouts and spoke up in defense of David before Saul. When David had to flee, he brought Jonathan into his confidence.

This friendship indicates that, in the end, openness and trust must reign between friends. This is similarly explained by Moses, with whom God spoke in the Tent of Meeting "face to face, as one speaks to a friend" (Exodus 33:11). Here the Greek translation reads: "As a man speaks to his friend." As Greek thought and sensibilities encroach upon those of Israel, more is said about friendship. Thus it is no wonder that we find an inspirational song about friendship in the late book known as the Wisdom of Jesus ben Sirach:

The Gift of Friendship

Faithful friends are a sturdy shelter:
   whoever finds one has found a treasure.
Faithful friends are beyond price;
   no amount can balance their worth.
Faithful friends are life-saving medicine;
   and those who fear the Lord will find them.
Those who fear the Lord direct their friendship aright,
   for as they are, so are their neighbors also.

(Sirach 6:14–17)

But friendship is also a gift that wants to be attained and proven reliable.

When you gain friends, gain them through testing,
   and do not trust them hastily.
For there are friends who are such when it suits them,
   but they will not stand by you in time of trouble.
And there are friends who change into enemies,
   and tell of the quarrel to your disgrace.
And there are friends who sit at your table,
   but they will not stand by you in time of trouble.

(Sirach 6:7–10)

These are words of wisdom, behind which stand life experiences. It is necessary to find a good and true friend.

Who can be a friend to me according to today's standard? Perhaps a neighbor whom I know, a confidant with whom I can speak freely, a comrade who accompanies me through life. Consider the friendship that exists between women and men, between men and women. Human nearness, spiritual kinship, agreement in thoughts and feelings: these are the foundations of friendship.

Can one also have Jesus for a friend? It seems difficult when one considers the many centuries, the now-remote existence of the one who no longer dwells with us in bodily form, the alienation that comes as a result of his often harsh, indeed, hard words. Human nearness indeed presupposes that one is careful to listen for the trust-worthy sound of people's voices, discern their facial characteristics, and allow their words entry. Jesus is no longer within immediate reach in the same that as a person in the living present is; he has therefore become, to our sensibilities, foreign.

And yet Jesus can be my friend. He says the same to his disciples: "I do not call you servants any longer, because the servant does not know what the master is doing; but I have called you friends, because I have made known to you everything that I have heard from my Father" (John 15:15).

Jesus opens himself up to his friends; he offers the kind of candor that should reign between friends. He gives to them that which he and only he can give: the illuminating, blessed, and liberating words of God his father, who also can illumine our human existence and life. He knows that this is the very reason he was born and sent into the world, in order to bear witness to the truth (John 18:37). This is that truth by which alone one can live, that openness to the depth of our human existence that is laid bare before God. The friendship that Jesus offers flows from his very being. "You did not choose me but I chose you. And I appointed you to go and bear fruit, fruit that will last" (John 15:16). This is a friendship which bridges that remoteness, that gulf of time between us and the historical Jesus. Jesus is my present friend, whom I can hear when I am attentive to his word.

Friendship with Jesus

Just how such friendship can originate and appear is something I have experienced in a community that developed in Würzburg. This is the Aegidius[1] Community, which I came to know some years ago when a young woman called me and said: "You are always conducting worship in the St. Nicholas Home (a home for elderly and dependent persons); can't we also come sometime?" Naturally I responded with a hearty "yes."

Since then, members of the community, a group of committed laity, have come each Sunday, helping to arrange the service and taking care of the sick, the majority of whom are physically challenged. They also visit the occupants of the home, brightening up the early afternoon get-together with coffee and cake, planning outings, boating trips, and organized holiday retreats. Students comprise the majority of the community. There are persons studying to become teachers, lawyers, and doctors, and women and men from trade and service vocations besides. A sincere friendship unites them all, an expression of their friendship with Christ.

The first St. Aegidius Community originated in Rome in one of the poorest quarters (Trastevere) with a small church dedicated to the revered Aegidius. The community established a social center there, in which they offer a daily lunch for needy persons and make provisions for shelter. The members of this community, together with a constant influx of new members, desire nothing else but "to live the gospel."

When possible, people congregate daily for an evening worship service, where a passage from the Holy Scriptures is read that someone then interprets in context and applies to a concrete situation. In the middle of this scene stands Jesus, who is transported into our midst by way of the symbol of a candle on the altar. An icon directs our view to Jesus our friend with his holy mother. Through words and symbols Jesus exists in the midst of the community.

However, these mostly young Christians also engage themselves in the public sphere, entering thoroughly into political life. They cultivate active ecumenical contacts with other confessions and religious communities. The World Day of Prayer for Peace in Assisi 1986, in which Pope John Paul II took part, acted as a stimulus for further such meetings in Bari, in Malta and other places, and most recently in Milan in 1993 with Cardinal Martini. The community also organizes peace initiatives for overcoming factional feuds, vicious arguments, and hostility between peoples. It is essentially because of their efforts that the civil war in Mozambique was ended through a cease-fire and a peace agreement reached under the leadership of the Italian government.

Members of the community travel in eastern European countries seeking to make contact with the people living there, whether Christian or non-Christian, guided by an ideal that not a few young people today get enthused over, namely, abandonment of the use of force, making peace, bringing about community through reconciliation, kindness, and compassion. One must offer friendship and loving encounter directly to poor, physically challenged, sick, and lonely people in order to make life for them more bearable and worth living again. This is true not only for times and places of crisis but also for our day-to-day living together, rich and poor, haves and have-nots.

Only such an effort, one that grows out of the spirit of Jesus and tries to improve earthly conditions, can precipitate a trend of change in our society, dominated as it is by egotism and a lust for power. That is the very goal that the members of the Aegidius Community have set for themselves, a life ordered according to the gospel mandate. For the time being the community is above all engaged in efforts toward overcoming the cruel civil war in Rwanda, and we pray:

> O Lord, Father of all peoples, come to Africa to help in its many needs, and give special heed to the land of Rwanda, that the chain of vengeance and violent acts that devours the life of so many men and women may cease.

What moves me especially is the principle of friendship with Jesus. In the intercessory prayer after the Gospel, which the community members themselves composed, I hear again and again:

> Jesus, good friend, help the poor and forsaken!
> Jesus, good friend, heal the sick!
> Jesus, good friend, bring people together in love and unity.
> Jesus, good friend, have mercy on the evildoers and sinners!
> Jesus, good friend, give to us the peace that only you can give!

The Aegidius Community is a lay movement, an activity of young Christians who are changing the world by the spirit of Christ. They want to bring people together as brothers and sisters, making day-to-day life more humane. Their friendship with sick and elderly people—as well as people of other races and religions, and those who have been bowed over because of war and civil war, hunger and want—validates their friendship with Jesus, who gave himself for everyone. Out of friendship with Jesus grows contentment and joy in the midst of our fragmented and estranged society.

Friendship in Everyday Life

Jesus did not say much about friendship. However, in his parables he does describe some scenes of people living together in friendship, as, for example, in the parable of the persistently asking friend and, respectively, the eventually granting friend. "Suppose one of you has a friend, and you go to him at midnight and say to him, 'Friend, lend me three loaves of bread, for a friend of mine has arrived, and I have nothing to set before him.' And he answers from within, 'Do not bother me; the door has already been locked, and my children are with me in bed; I cannot get up and give you anything.' I tell you, even though he will not get up and give him anything because he is his friend, at least because of his persistence he will get up and give him whatever he needs" (Luke 11:5-8).

A persistent, stubborn friend! Jesus recounts an example from daily life, and he does not try to hide the fact that this kind of friendship can also be annoying. However, in the end the friend receives the help he is asking for, nothing less than the fulfillment of his request.

Parables should always teach the listener something. Here Jesus does not mean to say that we should ask impetuously, but rather that through persistent requesting we can attain something from God, who desires to hear and grant our requests. The linking words that Matthew also uses (7:7–11, from the Sayings Source Q) focus the prayer request upon God: "Ask, and it will be given you; search, and you will find; knock, and the door will be opened for you. For everyone who asks receives, and everyone who searches finds, and for everyone who knocks, the door will be opened. Is there anyone among you who, if your child asks for bread, will give a stone? Or if the child asks for a fish, will give a snake? If you then, who are evil, know how to give good gifts to your children, how much more will your Father in heaven give good things to those who ask him!" The Gospel of Luke (11:13) further varies these words: "If you then, who are evil, know how to give good gifts to your children, how much more will the heavenly Father give the Holy Spirit to those who ask him!"

The parables about the lost sheep and the lost drachma refer to another setting from everyday life. A man who has a hundred sheep, and then loses one, goes after the lost one, and when he has found it he puts it on his shoulders, calls his friends and neighbors together, and says to them: Rejoice with me; I have found my sheep again, the one that I lost. Similarly, a woman who has lost one of her ten drachmas searches and sweeps out her whole house until she finds the coin. When she finds it, she calls her female friends and neighbors together and says: Rejoice with me; I have recovered my drachma that I had lost.

In both parables we encounter portraits from daily life that one can vividly imagine. Jesus is telling them in order to describe to his hearers the joy God feels when people who have strayed away from him are found again. Here Jesus is not suggesting and recommending friendship in everyday life; but it is presupposed and it illustrates the relationship of God to people who are far removed from him.

Furthermore, Jesus knows quite well the art of directing attention to negative examples from which he extrapolates examples of correct behavior for his disciples. "But when you are invited, go and sit down at the lowest place, so that when your host comes, he may say to you, 'Friend, move up higher'; then you will be honored in the presence of all who sit at the table with you" (Luke 14:10). Jesus observes the aspiration for the most honored seats and wants to encourage his disciples to practice humility and prudence. When the host referred to here addresses a guest as "my friend," we catch a glimpse of Jesus turning to the disciples as his friends, wishing to urge them in the direction of correct behavior. Jesus also urges against inviting friends in order to gain a return. "He said also to the one who had invited him, 'When you give a luncheon or a dinner, do not invite your friends or your brothers or your relatives or rich neighbors, in case they may invite you in return, and you would be repaid. But when you give a banquet, invite the poor, the crippled, the lame, and the blind. And you will be blessed, because they cannot repay you, for you will be repaid at the resurrection of the righteous'" (Luke 14:12–14).

This text makes it immediately clear what Jesus understands friendship to be. Motivated by God's love toward all of humankind, Jesus is setting up a new social order: from the first the friends of God and Jesus are the people who are overlooked and undervalued. In the Sermon on the Mount this claim of God is made even stronger: "If you do good to those who do good to you, what credit is that to you? For even sinners do the same. If you lend to those from whom you hope to receive, what credit is that to you? Even sinners lend to sinners, to receive as much again" (Luke 6:33f.). This connects naturally with the commandment to love one's enemies.

Similarly, Jesus has observed friendship among people; he has in no way disregarded or excluded it; much to the contrary, he has placed it on a higher level. True friendship must be seen in the light of the friendship that God imparts to people, and it sets new standards. Jesus actualized this in his person and offered a friendship to people that transcended all that had gone before. He sat at table with well-known tax collectors despised as sinners on account of their often fraudulent behavior (Mark 2:15), and he defended this table fellowship against narrow-minded scribes (2:16f.). Indeed, he did not reject the woman at a banquet who washed his feet, dried them with her hair, and anointed them with costly ointment, even though she was recognized as a city prostitute. He accepted her to-ken of love and held it up to Simon, the host, shaming him in front of everyone (Luke 7:36–50). What the woman did sprang forth from her love and her contrition over her sins. This presupposes that she was already gripped by the goodness and compassion of Jesus and sought his friendship. Just what friendship with Jesus means is made clear in the effusive love of this woman and in Jesus' reaction to her. Jesus says to her, "Your sins are forgiven you"; by this he is including her in the joy and friendship of God.

Friendship is not discussed explicitly in these connections; but when love is manifested in this way, then it is an expression of friendship. To be sure, such friendship has transcended all erotic feelings. All malicious insinuations about Jesus with regard to this woman or Mary Magdalene are mere fabrications and groundless; furthermore, the identification of this woman with Mary Magdalene does not hold up. Such an interpretation depends on a false connec-tion with Mary Magdalene (who is mentioned later, in 8:2), out of whom seven demons had gone. We will have more to say about Mary Magdalene a little further on.

Friendship in Persecutions and Afflictions

Jesus also warned his friends that they would face persecutions and sufferings unto death. In Luke 12:4 he explicitly addresses the disciples as friends, confronting them with the matter of destined death: "I tell you, my friends, do not fear those who kill the body, and after that can do nothing more." He is reminding them that God alone holds the power to throw human beings into eternal destruc-tion. It is not humans that they should fear but rather God, who can take eternal life away from them. However, they are kept safe by the power and watchful care of God! "Are not five sparrows sold for two pennies? Yet not one of them is forgotten in God's sight. But even the hairs of your head are all counted. Do not be afraid" (12:6).

Friendship with Jesus removes all fear of death and all of the terror of martyrdom. There is a vast stream of women and men who have been martyred, who through their witness for Christ overcame their horror of torture and execution. Ignatius, the bishop of Antioch who was sentenced to death at the beginning of the second century, wrote the Romans while awaiting his execution: "I write to all the churches and certify to all that I die willingly for God provided you not hinder me. I exhort you: do not become an inopportune kindness for me; let me be the food of wild beasts . . . ; I am the wheat of God, and I am ground by the teeth of wild beasts that I may be found pure bread" (Ignatius, *To the Romans* 4.1).[2]

Polycarp, the venerated teacher and bishop of Smyrna, bore a similar witness in the middle of the second century: he was publicly burned to death at the age of eighty-six. A detailed report of the community informs us of the events surrounding his martyrdom. When the proconsul offered him the opportunity for freedom if he would blaspheme Christ, he said: "Eighty-six years I have served him, and he has never done anything wrong to me; how could I now blaspheme my king, who has formed me?"

In more recent times there have occurred many persecutions of Christians in missionary lands, those who bore witness to their belief and their faithfulness to Christ. This was the case when in 1597 twenty-six Japanese Christians were crucified, and when in 1622 martyrdom came to many in Nagasaki. Sacrificial blood was spilled also in China and Korea, and again in Uganda, where in 1885 twenty-two black Christians suffered death. Scarcely a land was exempt from this type of blood toll. But the blood of the martyrs was the seed from which a new Christian reality grew. The living power of Christianity proved itself many times over through the readiness of the disciples of Christ to die. The history of all Christian persecutions has not yet been written. It would not only verify the word of Christ, "If they persecuted me, they will [also] persecute you" (John 15:20); it would also explicate the motives for martyrdom.

In our century, the records of the great persecutions in the areas under communist rule are quite impressive. Christians spoke a clear message through what they related in the Bolshevik courts before being transported to the penal colonies in Siberia, in the "Gulag Archipelago." The Baptist pastor Georgi P. Vins, who was fiercely persecuted along with his whole family, said in his final word to the judges in the 1966 trial: "You regard us here neither as thieves nor as robbers. Today, as in the time of Pilate, Christ the Savior is accused. Once again there is mocking and scorn, slander and noisy jubilance. But he remains yet, and his glance embraces sinners with unending compassion."

In his closing remarks of his defense, a chemical engineer, who was sentenced to three years of grueling forced labor, said, "Oh no, you cannot destroy the faith. Your efforts are to no avail in imprisoning Christ. The triumph of his suffering continues in us, whom he has saved."

Young Christians from Siberia write to the brothers and sisters in the West, "There is only one immeasurably great blue sky over us and over you. One heaven where our beloved friend Jesus waits, and where we soon shall meet at his feet. Until this reunion in heaven, friends!" (from the journal *pro fratribus*, Cologne).

Friendship with Jesus provides the power for survival and the certainty of victory over indifference, loneliness, scorn, and scoffing during the nearly endless time of imprisonment and forced labor. It enables one to prevail over the abuses of atheists, as we also today experience them, where people do not want any more to do with Christ and the church. Also today, friendship with Jesus acts as a rejuvenating spark, stirring enthusiasm and commitment in matters of faith, readiness to serve suffering people, and personal devotion.

Friendship with Jesus in Sickness and Frailty

It is not only distress and persecution from without that necessitate true friendship with Jesus, leading to a devoted life, but also sicknesses that are imposed on us, sufferings and testings that happen to us during the course of our life. Actually, this is the most likely scenario in which our friendship with Jesus must prove itself valid. Whoever lies in the sickbed, or is threatened by an incurable illness, will likely come to consider what will become of him, and when and how God will someday call him away. These are probing questions that haunt the sufferer, clouding his or her very life.

Then the sufferer may not only sigh, and call on God for help, but also quarrel, as Job does, with God: "I loathe my life; I will give free utterance to my complaint; I will speak in the bitterness of my soul. I will say to God, 'Do not condemn me; let me know why you contend against me' " (Job 10:1–2). "I loathe my life; I would not live forever. Let me alone, for my days are a breath" (7:16). Job struggles with the incomprehensible ways of God; he does not understand why God might severely chastise one who has dealt justly and served him faithfully.

In spite of everything, in the end Job bends his knee before the power and wisdom of God, and yet an answer concerning the sufferings of the righteous eludes him. Every person facing severe illness wrestles with thoughts like those of the suffering Job that may harass him or her again and again; further, I understand that at that point death is sometimes longed for. Nevertheless we must say to ourselves in all trials: if God grants you life, it means that you must persevere and surrender to God's will.

But how can we find consolation amid such outer and inner sufferings? The New Testament provides an answer here: Even Jesus, the Son of God, took upon himself this pain, affirming the way of the cross, and said to God in his darkest hour: "Remove this cup from me; yet, not what I want, but what you want" (Mark 14:36). Looking up to the Father (Abba), he withstood his hour of mortal fear.

The example of Jesus is in itself a great encouragement and comfort, because God saved the crucified One and raised him to new life. This familiar thought receives fresh illumination when we view Jesus as our friend, the friend who accompanies us along the path of suffering and dying. In hours of great need and distress I can turn to and pray to him for strength and resignation. He is near to us; he leads us through all periods of darkness and desperation. Jesus is a true friend who understands us and inwardly strengthens us.

How often have I experienced this at the bedside of a believer in league with Christ! It is indeed a great help when others, out of their friendship with Jesus, stand together to the very end with the suffering and dying, empathizing and showing solidarity with them through closeness and friendship. Jesus, my friend, is a helper in all of the situations of life, especially those where people have become bereft of counsel and can find no way of escape.

Chapter 6
Friendship according to John and Paul

rom the Gospel of John one may deduce how Jesus' friendship is seen and valued. The Fourth Gospel took the Hellenistic concept of friendship and brought it into the Christian arena.

John the Baptist

Jesus connected with John the Baptist from the start, and he acknowledged him as a witness for himself, designating him once as his friend. Jesus obtains the first disciples out of the company of John's disciples, and even though an argument erupts between John's disciples and some Jews over the matter of purification, John holds selflessly to the friendship. He describes himself as the friend who leads the people to Jesus, employing the metaphor of the bride-announcer who leads the bride to the bridegroom. The friend rejoices with the bridegroom who has found his bride—which here is the holy community. John is not the Messiah, but he helps to gather the sacred community. His joy is now great because the people have rushed to Jesus. He abdicates to Jesus, the Messiah, withdrawing completely, and is still able to rejoice selflessly over Jesus' success. He says humbly: "He must increase, but I must decrease" (3:30).

Jesus recognized the Baptist's friendship and valued it highly, as a word out of the Logion source confirms: "Among those born of women no one has arisen greater than John the Baptist; yet the least in the kingdom of heaven is greater than he" (Matthew 11:11/Luke 7:28).

Mary, Martha, and Lazarus

Friendship grows out of love. A covenant of love binds Jesus to Mary, Martha, and Lazarus, who lived in Bethany near Jerusalem and with whom Jesus quite often stayed. "Jesus loved Martha, her sister, and Lazarus" (John 11:5). As Lazarus grew seriously ill the two sisters sent the message: "Lord, your friend is sick." At first glance it seems strange that Jesus did not rush immediately to Lazarus's sickbed, but rather "he stayed two days longer in the place where he was" (11:6). In the meantime Lazarus died. Jesus' behavior can hardly be explained except by supposing that he wanted to perform an even greater wonder on his friend: resurrection from death. Jesus says, "This sickness is not to the death; rather it is for God's glory so that the Son of God may be glorified through it" (11:4).

For John the resurrection of Lazarus from death is, however one may explain it, a deeply symbolic occurrence, a proof of Jesus' power over death. Jesus weeps in front of Lazarus's tomb, whereupon the Jews say, "See how he loved him!" (11:35f.). The quite graphic, indeed dramatically narrated history is a visible manifestation of Jesus' power. He has life to bestow, not only physical but rather, above and beyond that, divine eternal life that even survives death. It is noteworthy that this revelation was granted to the loving and believing siblings from Bethany. Martha is the believing one who fully and completely affirms Jesus' words. Mary is the loving one who is shaken to her very depths, bewailing the death of her brother (11:33). Lazarus is the one in whom the wonder of the resurrection of the dead occurs, which thereby becomes a symbol of bestowed life. And yet the miracle is also a sign of that special love Jesus had for

Mary, Martha, and Lazarus. At the anointing later in Bethany, Mary shows herself to be the loving one who anoints Jesus with costly oil in preparation for his burial (12:1–8). The various traditions about the siblings in Bethany are condensed in John as a story of the friendship and love of Jesus. Love and belief are the prerequisites for a true and deep friendship.

Peter and the Disciple Whom Jesus Loved

Friendship with Jesus can take different forms, as is shown by the relationship of Jesus to both Peter and "the disciple whom Jesus loved," each of whom plays a significant role in John's Gospel. Peter, as one of the first disciples to be called by Jesus, wants to give his all for Jesus, even to sacrifice his life for him (13:37). Yet he deceives himself by not taking his human weakness into account. In the hour of testing he denies Jesus three times (18:17–18, 25–27).

One must compare this scene before the Passion with another that is set after the resurrection of Jesus: at the appearance of the risen One at the Sea of Galilee, Jesus asks the disciple, "Simon, son of John, do you love me more than these?" And Peter answers: "Yes, Lord; you know that I love you." Jesus asks another two times, whereupon Peter becomes sad because of Jesus' having thrice repeated the question "Do you love me?" (21:17). Peter perceives in this a reminder of his own denial, but he is also feels that Jesus has forgiven his failure, granting his love to him yet again. Of course, Jesus also prophesies to him concerning his future destiny: "When you were younger, you used to fasten your own belt and to go wherever you wished. But when you grow old, you will stretch out your hands, and someone else will fasten a belt around you and take you where you do not wish to go" (21:18). The evangelist remarks that Jesus wanted to indicate to him the manner of death by which he would glorify God.

This relationship of the apostle Peter to Jesus reflects an animated story of friendship with Jesus. Peter's calling threatens to founder on his human failings. Jesus, however, does not allow him to fall. Ultimately he reinstates Peter to his office: "Feed my lambs, feed my sheep!" (21:15-17). In spite of Peter's breach of trust, Jesus maintains his love and friendship toward him.

The other, unnamed disciple, "the disciple whom Jesus loved," is probably a man from Jerusalem who was with Jesus both at the cross and at his death (19:35). His friendship with Jesus never seems to have wavered. He was Jesus' confidant, who rested upon his breast at the Last Supper (13:23; 21:20), and to whom Jesus disclosed his inner life. This disciple was probably the head of the whole Johannine circle. It is a deep friendship, founded by Jesus, that this disciple proved himself worthy of. Both friends of Jesus, Peter and the beloved disciple, have their place by his side, and each was called to his own special task. The disciple whom Jesus loved is, for the Johannine community, the prototype of the loving disciple, the unwavering friend to whom Jesus can entrust himself.

There are different types of friendship: a friendship that consists of untarnished accord, and also another friendship that knows tensions but nevertheless remains firm. The relationship of the beloved disciple to Jesus counts as the first form of friendship; the broken relationship between Peter and Jesus counts as the second. Jesus accepts them both in their difference. Friendship with Jesus is a school of love. Although Peter only later arrives at a belief in the risen One, his love for Jesus is no less heartfelt. At Jesus' appearance on the sea, after hearing from the beloved disciple that it is the Lord, Peter lays aside his outer garment and jumps into the water in order to reach him (21:7).

In this story there are yet other enigmatic thoughts, chiefly in the description of the community of disciples that recognized the risen One at the bounteous fish catch and then had a meal with him. But in these narratives, replete with symbols, Peter and the disciple whom Jesus loved each played his own role. The circle of friends of Jesus is established, becoming the Johannine community.

Mary Magdalene

Yet another figure plays a special role in the Easter story: Mary Magdalene. She is the grand loving one who stands with other women at the cross (19:25) and does not want to separate herself from her beloved Lord after his death. She searches for the body of Jesus and, not finding it, she runs to Simon Peter and the beloved disciple and reports to them, trembling, that someone has taken the Lord away from the tomb (20:1f.). While the disciples "again returned to the house," Mary Magdalene "stood outside in front of the tomb and wept." Overcome with grief, she just stays at the tomb. Next follow scenes that demonstrate better than anything the woman's profound commitment to Jesus. The risen One appears to her, calling to her: "Mary!" At the sound of the voice she recognizes that it is Jesus and answers him: "Rabbouni!" which means Master, which is without doubt the way she referred to him during his earthly life (20:14-16).

From this scene contemporary readers have drawn sexual and erotic meanings, reaching fantastic conclusions: that Mary would have been the secret lover of Jesus, perhaps representing the woman he married and lived with again after his ostensible death! However, Mary Magdalene, from whom Jesus according to Luke 8:2 "had cast out seven demons," keeps her distance in spite of her love for Jesus. "Rabbouni" is no erotic term of endearment, rather a title for the teacher whom she gratefully admires. He also gives her a similar missionary commission: "But go to my brothers [the disciples] and say to them, 'I am ascending to my Father' " (John 20:17).

Mary Magdalene did not cultivate a special friendship with Jesus. She belonged to the circle of Jesus' brothers and sisters, the gathered Christian community. Furthermore, she is not depicted as a converted sinner, but rather as a woman who was delivered from serious illness. Her identification with the "sinner-woman" who anointed Jesus' feet in Luke 7, as well with the Mary from Bethany, is nothing but legend. In the Middle Ages it was said that Mary

Magdalene, along with Martha and Lazarus, had gone to Provence and that they were buried there. Coming from a good home, she was a harlot who was converted by Jesus. She served him at a banquet and stood firm with him at his crucifixion and death. A pious romance!

The last facts reported by the Gospels about Mary Magdalene, that she stood among the women at the cross, was present at the burial, and then experienced an appearance of the risen One, are enough for us to recognize her as a true, loving disciple. Her friendship with Jesus extends beyond the grave. In Mary Magdalene we see an utterly trusting, personal, and profoundly spiritual friendship—an exemplary relationship—being cast in bold relief before all Christians.

The Circle of Friends in the Johannine Community

Friendship also continued in the community of believers that rose up after the death and resurrection of Jesus, in the form of beliefs and relationships. Paradoxically, it was bolstered by the emergence of false teachers in the Johannine community. The Johannine letters provide insight into these tensions, which developed out of the community schism between those who held to a belief in Jesus as the Messiah and Son of God, and those who interpreted Jesus differently. The latter were particularly fervent in rejecting notions of Jesus' coming "in the flesh," "by water and blood," and also of his expiatory crucifixion (1 John 4:2,10; 5:6). A whole group of these unorthodox believers would separate themselves from the community. "They went out from us, but they did not belong to us; for if they had belonged to us, they would have remained with us. But by going out they made it plain that none of them belongs to us" (1 John 2:19).

The author of this weighty epistle of John, certainly a leading man from the Johannine circle, sees them as "antichrists," enemies of Jesus (1 John 2:18–22; 2 John 7). He associates all the more with those who share the same belief in the Son of God become human and who prove themselves genuine through their love for the brethren and sisters. It is for that very reason that he offered a notion of friendship like that which we find in the third epistle of John. Here the author, "the elder" from the Johannine circle, has to battle with yet another adversity.

In the community where a man named Gaius lives, to whom the letter is addressed, there resided a unenlightened and domineering leader of the community named Diotrephes. He wanted to keep itinerant missionaries who were endorsed by the "elder" away from the community, and to exclude those of the community who would accept these missionaries. With biting words Diotrophes stirred up strife against the "elder" and shut his friends out of the community (3 John 10). However, the "elder" encouraged Gaius to prolong his show of host friendship to the traveling missionaries. As the letter ends, he speaks about his friends who stayed with him. "The friends send you their greetings. Greet the friends there, each by name" (3 John 15).

Friendship between believing brothers is not to be taken for granted. True friends stick together and support all who need their help. Their actions will be determined only by the tasks that Jesus has charged them to accomplish. To be sure, today's church contains narrow-minded officeholders. And yet overflowing charity and love toward all are signs that Jesus' commission and message are understood after all. Tradition holds that Jesus rebuked his disciples when they wanted to hinder a man who was casting out demons in his name. John said to him, "Teacher, we saw someone casting out demons in your name, and we tried to stop him, because he was not following us." But Jesus said, "Do not stop him; for no one who does a deed of power in my name will be able soon afterward to speak evil of me. Whoever is not against us is for us" (Mark 9:38–40). This word can be considered as an ecumenical principle. Wherever and however good is done, Jesus acknowledges it.

Friendship with Jesus becomes a personal friendship in the Johannine community. The letter writer hopes to see the friends soon, and to speak with them "mouth to mouth."[1] Friendship with Christ leads to friendship between one other, as the exegete Jürgen Roloff has stated in his new, impressive work about "The Church in the New Testament." The Johannine portion is given the striking heading: "The Society of the Friends of Jesus."

Friendship as Becoming One with Christ and in Christ

Whoever wishes to understand friendship with Jesus in its deeper dimensions must take in this thought, which is equally demonstrated in Paul and in John: Friendship with Jesus is an inner union with the suffering and risen Christ and a rootedness in the Holy Spirit that is granted to us, making us free children of God. Through his sufferings, which he accepts in the service of Jesus Christ, Paul knows existentially that he has been caught up in the suffering and death of Jesus. "We are afflicted in every way, but not crushed; perplexed, but not driven to despair; persecuted, but not forsaken; struck down, but not destroyed; always carrying in the body the death of Jesus, so that the life of Jesus may also be made visible in our bodies" (2 Corinthians 4:8–10).

In afflictions, persecutions, and sufferings, Paul becomes completely one with Jesus, who had to go the bitter way to the cross. Without doubt Paul sees himself included in these sufferings with Jesus that he might share in the attainment of his resurrection. "I want to know Christ and the power of his resurrection and the sharing of his sufferings by becoming like him in his death" (Philippians 3:10).

This becoming one with Christ, even in suffering, was called "Passion mysticism." "Mysticism" is a polyvalent and difficult concept to grasp, but it does a good job of conveying the very intimate, internal experience of becoming one with Christ, who is the present and active friend of the soul. We unite, so to speak, with this friend, so that his feelings become our feelings and our feelings become his experience.

It is likely that not all friends of Jesus Christ will ascend to this height, because that requires the very living circumstances of the afflicted apostle, which Paul often described in his catalogs of suffering. Paul was often in prison, beaten, in danger of death. "Five times I have received from the Jews the forty lashes minus one. Three times I was beaten with rods. Once I received a stoning. Three times I was shipwrecked; for a night and a day I was adrift at sea" (2 Corinthians 11:23–25). The fruits of all these difficult trials for Jesus' sake come from drawing upon the strength of Jesus through self-immersion in Jesus' mortal sufferings. Moreover, all of us can have some idea of what it means to become one with Christ and his destiny.

To become one with Christ is to exist in Christ. Paul speaks to this issue in one place: "I have been crucified with Christ; and it is no longer I who live, but it is Christ who lives in me. And the life I now live in the flesh I live by faith in the Son of God, who loved me and gave himself for me" (Galatians 2:19f.). In a personal way, the apostle sees himself as loved by Christ who gave himself for him. If we ask how becoming one with Christ and in Christ can be possible, we are referred to the Holy Spirit. "God's love has been poured into our hearts through the Holy Spirit that has been given to us" (Romans 5:5). It is through gaining assurance in the love of God that we secure a new relationship to God as our father. We become his sons and daughters and are freed from all slavery.

But how do we attain this relationship, this awareness that we are God's children? Through the Holy Spirit, who cries within us "Abba! Father!" (Galatians 4:6). Paul accepts this witness of the Spirit within us as fully real: "You have received a spirit of adoption. When we cry, 'Abba! Father!' it is that very Spirit bearing witness with our spirit that we are children of God" (Romans 8:15f.). To be sure, we can only obtain such an experience of the Spirit through prayer.

The presence of the Spirit can become real to us in personal as well as in corporate prayer. Having our prayer spiritually fulfilled is not easily accomplished, though, when we have been distracted by our day-to-day concerns and unfocused thoughts. Paul knew this also: "We do not know how to pray as we ought, but that very Spirit intercedes with sighs too deep for words. And God, who searches the heart, knows what is the mind of the Spirit, because the Spirit intercedes for the saints according to the will of God" (Romans 8:26f.).

These represent the prayer experiences that Paul himself had. He points to them in order to encourage the kind of praying that he wants all Christians to practice. We need only believe in the Spirit, which lives in our heart and supplements what our prayer lacks. What we want to say to God is more a sigh, indeed a groan, that the Holy Spirit takes and God makes understandable. The human spirit and the divine spirit are linked together in a language that God, who investigates the heart, understands, even if it is only a stammer and a sigh. One can also call this mystical prayer, to which belongs silent reflection, self-immersion in the love of God, and the entrusting of self to the Holy Spirit. All the great saints prayed in this way, and to be sure also many "minor souls," as perhaps the venerated Theresia of the Child Jesus, who discovered in Jesus her brother and friend.

If we seek friendship with Jesus, this prayer guidance is a way to it. In the dryness and drought of our spirits, all of us, including young people, can travel this way to find the ever-new source of life and the light of joy, even amid all the disruption of our time. Because in God is "the fountain of life, in [his] light we see light" (Psalm 36:9).

After prayer orientation focused on Paul, we will now have a look at the Gospel of John, where our unity with Christ is brought out in another way: through him we can experience a descent into God.[2] John directs everything back to the love of God, which is made available to us in Jesus Christ. "For God so loved the world that he gave his only Son, so that everyone who believes in him may not perish but may have eternal life" (John 3:16). Jesus reveals to us the lifegiving love of God. Everything that he heard from his Father he revealed to his friends (15:15). This is none other than the love with which God wished to call the world, which had shut itself off from him, back to himself. The revelation of the Son brings about the result that we are included in the living existence of the Son with the Father. It is Jesus alone whom we can thank that we are now caught up in the flow of God's love.

Therefore Jesus is able to say, using the vivid metaphor of the grapevine and the branches, "I am the true vine, and my Father is the vinegrower" (15:1). Through his word we are made pure. "Abide in me as I abide in you" (v. 4). "Those who abide in me and I in them bear much fruit, because apart from me you can do nothing" (v. 5). Through this the Father is glorified, and everything that we ask him for is given to us (vv. 7-8).

Here also, as in Paul, it is a matter of prayer and its fulfillment, which occurs through the Holy Spirit. The Spirit carries our requests to God through our association with Jesus, which assures us of rich productivity. In John it is also ultimately the Holy Spirit who makes this harvest of love possible. At his departure Jesus says to his disciples, "And I will ask the Father, and he will give you another Advocate, to be with you forever. This is the Spirit of truth, whom the world cannot receive, because it neither sees him nor knows him. You know him, because he abides with you, and he will be in you" (14:16f.).

Let us pause here, in order to consider what these words of the Bible mean for our prayers! The friendship prayer with Jesus, as it is practiced by the Aegidius Community mentioned earlier, is a prayer to the Father in and through the Holy Spirit. Our friendship and association with Jesus does not become efficacious through us and our human cries, but rather through the power of the Spirit, which flows toward us as branches in the grapevine of Christ. I would like to encourage everyone to practice such prayers. In the Aegidius Community we make a special point of including the sick and those undergoing trials of suffering, the elderly and the lonely, the poor and the needy in our prayers.

At the ecumenical prayer conferences, where we show solidarity with other religious communities, we still emphasize praying: for peace in the world; against the prevalence of group egotism and hate; for freedom from violence and every kind of oppression. It is part of Jesus' message that hate and persecution would come from the unbelieving world; however, to his friends he affirms, "In the world you face persecution. But take courage; I have conquered the world!" (16:33). Consequently, we have freedom in the midst of a fragmented world. "So you have pain now; but I will see you again, and your hearts will rejoice, and no one will take your joy from you" (16:22). These farewell words of Jesus to his true disciples refer to the joy that they will experience in the new encounter with Jesus, the resurrected One. In fact, a deep inner joy springs from prayer that we, in unity with Jesus, pray with an upward gaze to the Father. People who give their friendship with Jesus expression through bearing fruit in love and immersion in prayer are happy, worry-free people.

In the magnificent prayer to the Father, the so-called high-priestly prayer (John 17), Jesus includes everything that he wants to say to "his own" in regard to his earthly work—and also their future. "I have made your name known to those whom you gave me from the world" (17:6). By that is meant his friends who have understood that he came from the Father. He asks for them that they be kept safe in the fellowship with him and the Father. It is a caring prayer for all who remain near to him through faith. He protected them so that none of them was lost except the son of perdition, the betrayer, that the scripture might be fulfilled (17:12).

Like Jesus, his disciples also encounter the world's animosity. He does not want them to leave the world; on the contrary, he sends them into the world (17:18) and asks only that they be kept safe from the evil one. He is consecrated for them, offering himself through devotion unto death. Jesus prays for yet one more special thing: that they might become one, as the Father is in the Son and the Son in the Father. They can therefore be one in him, "as you, Father, are in me and I am in you" (17:21).

To abide in Jesus is to keep his commands. That is reciprocal love. "If you keep my commandments, you will abide in my love, just as I have kept my Father's commandments and abide in his love" (15:10). "This is my commandment, that you love one another as I have loved you" (15:12). Jesus' love for his friends is bound to continue, proving its worth through mutual love.

Can we still promote these lofty convictions today? A prerequisite for that is a portrait of Jesus Christ that unites the characteristics of the historical Jesus with those of his present living power. His whole life was a "pro-existence," a life for the other to the point where he became consumed for others. One does not need to view him as a "superstar," but rather as a onetime, extraordinary phenomenon. Today's meandering, perverse—indeed ludicrous—reconstructions of Jesus Christ cannot distort and obliterate his true personage as it confronts us in the Gospels. What can be said against a claim like this, that Jesus did not really die, but rather he was perhaps healed by Qumran Essenes and made a living comeback? Or that he married Mary Magdalene and had children with her? Purely delusional portraits, which today's authors concoct because they cannot understand that even in his harshness Jesus is borne along by a great love. They want to typecast Jesus as laid-back, falsely attributing romantic relationships to him that find no resonance in the Gospels whatever.

The true portrait of Jesus is a completely different one: It shows the great friend of humanity who heals the sick and takes care of the poor, who stands up against the rulers and powers, and who goes to his death because of his message of the coming kingdom of God. Filled with this Spirit, innumerable persons have followed him, devoting themselves and wearing themselves out in love. They have experienced friendship with Jesus in the Holy Spirit together with that inner joy which comes as a result of following him. Friendship and oneness with Christ lead to a new adventure of love, devotion to humanity, and the joy that grows out of it. By this experience, notwithstanding our skeptical and often joyless contemporary experience, everyone—especially young people—can become newly inspired.

Chapter 7
Jesus as the Model for Humankind

 e seldom view Jesus as truly human, as a person who lived among people as we do, who wanted to move them toward a truer humanity and humaneness.[1] For a long time, Catholic religious piety venerated Jesus above all as the Son-of-God-become-human, as the "Lord God on the cross," who delivered us. Even in dogmatics, Jesus stood centrally as the Son of God on earth, worker of mighty deeds. It could be seen as a step forward when the Tübingen dogmatic theologian Karl Adam proposed that believers focus on Christ as our brother.[2] Christ should be seen not only as the divine deliverer enthroned at the right hand of the Father but also as one bonded with us, the firstborn among many brethren. Otherwise his human friendliness, totally encompassing love, and human nearness are slighted. For although we know Jesus as God and man, we must take his humanity seriously. If we see him mainly as judge over our actions, the one before whom we must give account, then, Adam asserts, the religion of love becomes a religion of fear, as the history of sacral architecture indeed indicates: "In order to give outward expression to the new sense of remoteness from the eucharistic God, the altar is withdrawn from the gaze of the people, first by means of curtains, and later by the painted wooden partition of the iconostasis. The eucharistic sacrifice has come to be regarded as essentially the awful mystery, and if it still preserves something of the attractiveness of mystery, that element is only faintly discernible" (*Christ Our Brother*, 50-51).

In contrast with that sense of remoteness from God, Karl Adam called attention to Jesus' humanity. His divinity is not the only, and for this day and time not the most important, aspect of Jesus' person. The spark in him is the appearance of the divine in the human. Jesus became our brother.

This picture of Jesus is witnessed to throughout the Gospels, but it especially stands out in the letter to the Hebrews. Christ does not hesitate to call people his brothers and sisters, saying: "I will proclaim your name to my brothers and sisters, in the midst of the congregation I will praise you" (Hebrews 2:11f.). "Therefore he had to become like his brothers and sisters in every respect, so that he might be a merciful and faithful high priest in the service of God, to make a sacrifice of atonement for the sins of the people" (2:17).

Jesus accepted all people as his brothers and his sisters. They became his friends also. How did the disciples experience Jesus as a human example? His serving devotion to people stands out. Bearing love and friendship, he devoted himself to the very ones who were ignored and pushed aside in contemporary society. For that he was reviled: "a friend of tax-collectors and sinners" (Luke 7:34); but Jesus is not put off by this. As for the prostitute at a banquet who washed his feet with her tears and anointed them with costly ointment, he defends her and shames Simon, the host (Luke 7:44–47). He tells the parable of the kindhearted father who unhesitatingly takes back the prodigal who was "lost," reinstating him in his rights as a son (Luke 15:16–32), much to the displeasure of the older son, who cannot get over the licentious life of his brother and has no desire to rejoice over the return home of the "one who was lost." Jesus rejoices over all who turn around and rediscover the love of God.

Jesus expresses his solidarity with all people, including the ignored, at the banquet with the tax collectors, who were at that time considered to be sinners because they were often frauds and nonobservers of Jewish law (Mark 2:13–17). His basic position is expressed in the phrase: "Those who are well have no need of a physician, but those who are sick." Jesus healed not only the physically sick but also the spiritually depressed who were plagued by their conscience and inwardly tormented, like the criminals crucified with him (Luke 23:40–43).

There are many examples of the compassion of Jesus with the marginalized, those bent over by sickness and sorrow. The woman who suffered many years with an issue of blood, who felt herself ostracized by the community because of her impurity, he accepts as "sister," as a full-fledged member of the holy people. Moreover he heals her of her disease (Mark 5:25-34). In Jesus' day and time there were many spiritual anomalies, deranged, possessed persons whose condition was attributed to the influence of evil spirits. Mark describes one such case in detail (5:1–20), where it concerns a man violently out of control, who had to live among the tombs away from inhabited areas. He met Jesus and was delivered from his torment. "[He was] sitting there, clothed and in his right mind" (5:15). Everything is described according to the conventions of the time, but the pith of the story centers on Jesus' healing, which bespeaks him as the quintessential therapist, even amid the most difficult of illness scenarios. This story can only be explained by recognizing Jesus' compassion for the beleaguered of humankind.

The story of the apparently epileptic servant, who, when falling to the ground during his attacks, would writhe, foam at the mouth, grind his teeth, and become rigid, is also striking (Mark 9:14–27). The hapless father begged Jesus' help: "If you are able to do anything, have pity on us and help us." The people thought that the youth was already dead; but "Jesus took him by the hand and lifted him up, and he was able to stand" (9:26f.).

One reads this story incorrectly if all one sees are extraordinary acts of wonder performed by Jesus, typecast as an archaic "divine" human. Clearly, mercy and the desire to help people are the motives that propelled Jesus to perform certain extraordinary deeds.

JESUS OUR FRIEND—A FASCINATING PORTRAIT

The widely attested healings and exorcisms of Jesus are also acknowledged today in science. In his critical work *The Miracle Stories of the Early Christian Tradition*,[3] Gerd Theissen states, "There is no doubt that Jesus worked miracles, healed the sick and cast out demons, but the miracle stories reproduce these historical events in an intensified form" (277). "As an apocalyptic charismatic miracle-worker, Jesus is unique in religious history" (278).

Jesus' disciples were witnesses to these miraculous healings. He chose them "to be with him, and to be sent out to proclaim the message, and to have authority to cast out demons" (Mark 3:14f.). He lived two or three years with them; he wanted to have them around as companions and confidants. They would be witnesses to the people of his healings, indeed also of other deeds: the stilling of the stormy sea, the feeding of the five thousand. He placed together persons from different origins and with different vocations in the circle of the twelve disciples, symbolic of the people created from the twelve tribes of Israel in its completed form under the rule of God. They included fishermen from the Sea of Galilee, a Zealot named Simon, and a man named Judas, probably from Judea, who later betrayed him. He accepted them all as his companions and messengers. Would they not have recognized his character in their close living association together?

Women also joined with him. They cared for part of his and his disciples' daily provisions (Luke 8:2–3). In this way he built up a circle of male and female friends who stayed close to him to the very end. The women followed him even to the cross, experienced his death with him, and took care of his sepulcher.

Jesus was therefore wholly human and lived among people. He ate and drank with them, traveled with them, and shared their difficult lot. Seldom would it have been a simple life, for Jesus once said to someone who wanted to follow after him, "Foxes have holes, and birds of the air have nests; but the Son of Man has nowhere to lay his head" (Luke 9:58).

With that we ask ourselves how Jesus could have become a human example for his disciples and friends. It may be said that his basic characteristic was selfless service, the fact that he excluded no one. What Jesus demanded and expected from his disciples he realized himself in his life.

Poverty

On one occasion Jesus exhorted his disciples, "Do not store up for yourselves treasures on earth, where moth and rust consume and where thieves break in and steal; but store up for yourselves treasures in heaven, where neither moth nor rust consumes and where thieves do not break in and steal" (Matthew 6:19f.). Actually, Jesus speaks often about money and possessions: "It will be hard for a rich person to enter the kingdom of heaven. Again I tell you, it is easier for a camel to go through the eye of a needle than for someone who is rich to enter the kingdom of God" (Matthew 19:23f.). Jesus was himself poor; he amassed no earthly treasure. His example was constantly observed by his disciples. Whoever followed after him gave up home and vocation and renounced worldly possessions. *Verba docent, exempla trahunt*—"Words instruct, examples carry along." Herein lies the secret of Jesus' intimates' fascination with him. They wanted nothing more than to live as he lived.

Singleness

Jesus renounced marriage and family; but he did not demand a slavish imitation of his style of living. According to Gospel reports, his imitators did not fully separate from their families. In this regard Paul is a good interpreter of Jesus' instructions: he himself was also unmarried, and he wished that many would be able to live as he did, without marriage or family. However, he felt free as an apostle and he did not want his communities to have to bear any added burden. "Do we not have the right to our food and drink? Do we not have the right to be accompanied by a believing wife, as do the other apostles and the brothers of the Lord and Cephas?" (1 Corinthians 9:4–5).

Accordingly, even after Jesus' death his believing followers lived in the normal way. Only on a freewill basis did individuals decide, like Paul, in favor of a celibate life. This is the source of questions regarding contemporary priestly celibacy, which the Catholic Church imposes as an obligation on candidates for the priesthood. Should not the church give its priests, too, the opportunity of choice between a life in marriage and family or in unmarried abstinence? It is a mistake to concretize for all time what in earlier centuries served as an ideal of full devotion in service to humanity.

Jesus conferred freedom on his disciples, and Paul followed him in this mode. The contemporary variety of living circumstances and societal perspectives can now perhaps allow for the positive concept of exemplary family life to appear, receiving its full worthy status. Jesus did indeed suggest to his disciples that they forego marriage "for the sake of the kingdom of heaven," but he made no commandment out of it. "Let anyone accept this who can" (Matthew 19:10–12). The renunciation of marriage can be a great thing, chosen in order to have the capability to serve with full freedom in the proclamation of God's kingdom. However it is not absolutely necessary, for today we see married deacons and pastoral assistants, who are accepted by the church.

Sacrificial Dedication

It is not a simple matter to follow Jesus' example in all things; But there are some requirements binding upon everyone. Among these are not only renouncing earthly treasures but also, and especially, forgoing all power and striving for dominance. In this respect Jesus is quite clear. He sees soberly and realistically what happens in the world because of power struggles and the oppression of others. "You know that among the Gentiles those whom they recognize as their rulers lord it over them, and their great ones are tyrants over them" (Mark 10:42).

Jesus as the Model for Humankind

The friends of Jesus must rid themselves entirely of the desire to rule. "But it is not so among you; but whoever wishes to become great among you must be your servant." Here Jesus is referring to his own service. He deliberately calls himself the "Son of Man," because he is the one who is coming once more with power, on the clouds of heaven, to judge the peoples according to their deeds, and to gather the elect from all directions (Mark 13:26f.). This very "Son of Man," chosen by God for power and authority, is the serving One during his time on earth, the slave of all, who even offers his life as a ransom for many (Mark 10:45). His service for humanity finds its zenith in his living sacrifice.

In John's Gospel, Jesus' service is demonstrated through the foot washing that he performs on his disciples at the Last Supper. "So if I, your Lord and Teacher, have washed your feet, you also ought to wash one another's feet. For I have set you an example, that you also should do as I have done to you" (John 13:14f.). Washing feet is not "a must" to be followed literally (as in the Maundy Thursday liturgy); it is much more an articulated picture of Jesus' devotion that led to self-sacrifice.

From this example, and from his association with Christ, Paul draws the conclusion that Christians should do nothing out of ambition or conceit, and he urges, "In humility regard others as better than yourselves. Let each of you look not to your own interests, but to the interests of others" (Philippians 2:3f.).

Many Christians have followed in the path of Jesus, that of a complete pro-existence, an existence for others. At one time, during the poverty movement of the Middle Ages, many people renounced worldly goods, and becoming infected by the love of the holy Franciscans, they also devotedly took care of the sick, in particular those with whom no one wished make contact, and those whom one would most likely push away. We hear that about the revered Elizabeth of Thuringia in the thirteenth century, who, abandoning her life in the Wartburg castle, went to the sick and took over the work with them that no one else wanted to do. Likewise today there are splendid examples of practical love in the footsteps of Jesus, such as those who care for lepers. Conspicuous is the sacrificial death of the Polish priest Maximilian Kolbe in the concentration camp at Auschwitz, who freely went and died in the bunker of hunger and death for a young family man. Many other known and unknown women and men were consumed in selfless willingness to act in behalf of the poor, sick, and dying, among whom are Mother Teresa and Abbé Pierre, the rag-and-bone man of Paris.

Power and oppression can be overcome through selfless service. The human example of Jesus is a standing incentive to live for others in a world of self-seeking and striving for wealth and domination, a world full of violence and oppression.

Tough Words against Being Unreasonable and Oppositional

To be sure, other characteristics are found in Jesus' person that demonstrate the limits of his mercy and forbearance. Certain people in the Israel of that day opposed Jesus with brutal severity and hard words—for example the teachers of the law, who by a narrow interpretation of the Jewish law totally obscured the love to be found there. When someone came to him on a Sabbath, bringing a man whose hand was withered, the teachers of the law paid close attention to see whether Jesus might heal on the Sabbath, which was forbidden according to the strict Sabbath regulations. Jesus asked them, " 'Is it lawful to do good or to do harm on the Sabbath, to save life or to kill?' But they were silent. He looked around at them with anger; he was grieved at their hardness of heart and said to the man, 'Stretch out your hand.' He stretched it out, and his hand was restored" (Mark 3:1–6).

Even though his acts for the wholeness and healing of people were met with hot hostility, still he would not be deterred from performing them. People also suspected that he drove out demons in league with Beelzebul, the prince of the demons—that is, magically, by association with demonic anti-divine powers. More than a few people today engage in such practices as devilish incantations, black masses, and other magical apparitions. Through the centuries, people have continued to hold even the most peculiar of these notions. With intellectual acumen, however, Jesus rejects all accusations that he has a covenant with Satan, and he states clearly that he breaks the spell of the demons only through the power of God (Mark 3:22–27). He has sharp words against accusations that would gainsay the power that he received from God: 'Truly I tell you, people will be forgiven for their sins and whatever blasphemies they utter; but whoever blasphemes against the Holy Spirit can never have forgiveness, but is guilty of an eternal sin'" (Mark 3:28f.). Jesus often upbraided this "adulterous and sinful generation" (Mark 8:12, 38); for the people were unbelieving (9:19), blind, and unrepentant.

The disciples experienced this seemingly harsh and grumbling Jesus also. They were bound to have been scolded by him and reminded that they themselves had a stubborn heart (Mark 8:17). They were like children who argue about who is the greatest among them. For this reason Jesus placed a child in their midst, took it in his arms and said to them: " 'Whoever welcomes one such child in my name welcomes me, and whoever welcomes me welcomes not me but the one who sent me'" (Mark 9:33-37).

The disciples should have learned early on that friendship with Jesus requires first of all an attitude of childlikeness before God, of self-effacement, and of high regard for despised and humble persons. With such object lessons he taught them to forego retaliation. When the disciples were refused entry into an inhospitable Samaritan village, they wanted to call down fire from heaven (Luke 9:52–55). Similarly, when they became upset that a foreign exorcist was casting out demons in the name of Jesus (Mark 9:38–40), he appealed to their forbearance and forgiveness.

Jesus' action is always the guiding principle for the disciples. In his way of thinking and manner of behavior he becomes for them the exemplar of humanity. No matter how often the disciples are timid in their human thoughts and disappoint him in their behavior, Jesus never gives up on his friendship with them.

More than a Human Example

Also worth considering is the fact that Jesus was not merely a human example for his disciples and friends. To the degree that he had fellowship with them, he still remained that Son-in-union-with-God who acted in the power of God, with whom they could never really be equal. A secret encased him in such a way that although he was indeed their friend, he was also an Other who remained inconceivable to them. In the jubilant acclamation to the Father he said, "All things have been handed over to me by my Father; and no one knows the Son except the Father, and no one knows the Father except the Son and anyone to whom the Son chooses to reveal him" (Matthew 11:27).

Jesus' greatest and darkest secret was his life's destiny, which, predetermined by the Father, necessitated his accepting suffering and death. This remained hidden to the disciples and evoked obvious misunderstanding and massive disagreement when Jesus revealed it to them. Peter took Jesus aside and reproached him because of his determination to walk the path of suffering. He even appealed to God, who surely could not wish this or allow it to occur. "God forbid it, Lord! May that never happen to you!" But Jesus repelled him as a tempter, as "Satan," and made it clear to him that he was not setting his mind on the thoughts of God, but rather on human notions. Thus there was a limit to the mutual understanding that was somehow related to Jesus' calling from God.

Jesus could not be a human example for his disciples in everything. Nevertheless it remains true that, despite the power conferred on him by God, and his clear authority already demonstrated on earth, he remains their friend and confidant. He is a model for them in every way; through both his word and his example he leads the way to humanity and humaneness.

Chapter 8
The Call for Decision

decision is required from each person who would enter into friendship with Jesus: to choose either the carefree, immoderate life of our pleasure- and status-seeking egotistical society, with its striving after reputation and positions of honor—or a life lived in behalf of others who are depressed because of poverty, sickness, and loneliness, who hope against hope that a selfless person full of loving devotion will come along. The latter gives precedence to striving after the inner fulfillment that comes in bringing others happiness. In the call for love is found the promise of a kingdom of endowment, gifts that the world is not able to give. "I have said these things to you so that my joy may be in you, and that your joy may be complete" (John 15:11). This inner joy is not obtained through the carefree, comfortable life in pursuit of this world's pleasure, but rather only if one is prepared through following the poor but internally contented Jesus in his sacrifice for others. This joy issues from love received and given again.

Peter once asked Jesus, "Look, we have left everything and followed you. What will we then have?" Upon hearing that, Jesus promised that Peter and the other disciples would be entitled to twelve thrones in order to judge the twelve tribes of Israel (Matthew 19:27f.). Accordingly they would hold special positions over the people of God in the kingdom rule of Jesus. Perhaps this privilege strikes us as a cheap promise that has in no way been fulfilled. Are not all of these promises (including the one where each person who "has left houses or brothers or sisters or father or mother or children or fields, for my name's sake, will receive a hundredfold, and will inherit eternal life"; Matthew 19:29) mirages that spring from Jesus' enthusiastic view of the future, but in the reality of the world burst like soap bubbles? I often hear it said that the prospects Jesus held out to his disciples and friends remain merely promises that no one can examine, and that in the course of history no one has yet seen them come to fruition. All exaggerated delusions, dreams, and whims! Have not the religious critics correctly concluded that these pictures of a better future, of a kingdom of God on earth, are projections as it were, wishful dreams of the not-yet-liberated human imagination? People are deceived by such, and are pacified, made to feel content by all the drama in a religious ceremony, by pretty words and empty promises. We recognize these thoughts and states of mind which have filled people's heads and hearts for a long time and do so especially today.

Is it truly worthwhile to seek friendship with Jesus, or are we chasing after a mirage, a chimera? To all friends—male and female—to whom I am bound in relationship with Jesus, I would like to say several things.

1. The joy that flows into our heart through our love for the sick, suffering, and lonely is no deception, for we experience it over and over again. Friendship with the oppressed, which we cultivate out of our friendship with Jesus, makes us more prosperous and fortunate, not because we have somehow been particularly "altruistic" people, but because we, through our actions, engender an experience in which all can share and thereby discover a deep dimension of our own human existence.

2. Jesus' promises to his followers and friends do not constitute utopian assurances concerning the future; rather, they are already grounded in the present. Certainly the final fulfillment in God's coming reign is yet to be, when heaven and earth pass away and this

old world is swallowed up. However, Jesus manifests uniqueness in that he preaches the inbreaking of the new creation and the holy powers it brings. These things are already present in his person and demonstrated through his works: the sick are healed, demons are cast out, the blind see again, the lame walk, lepers become clean, the deaf hear, the dead rise up (Matthew 11:5). This may be an inten- tionally universalized and intensified description of the healing deeds of Jesus, but we have already seen that behind it stands a real experience of his works as helper and physician of humankind. In these healing deeds humanity recognizes the divine activity that renews creation and human life and points to the world to come. After the healing of a deaf and dumb person the people praise God: "'He has done everything well; he even makes the deaf to hear and the mute to speak" (Mark 7:37). Creation, which God once declared to be good, is renewed, and led to its completion. This is a process that Jesus set into motion. The laws of creation are not violated, but an evolution toward betterment is initiated. God's kingly rule breaks in and rages against all evil, demonic pow- ers in this world. "But if it is by the finger of God that I cast out the demons, then the kingdom of heaven has come to you" (Luke 11:20).

3. The things that people strive after in the cold, loveless world— warmth, humanity, and humaneness—become reality through our friendship with Jesus and with the people whom we would include in that friendship. Success is possible even in a life of sickness and frailty, even in our death and the fear that goes along with it, all because of our participation in friendship with Jesus. No longer does fear eclipse our human existence and embitter our life. Love triumphs over suffer- ing, life over death.

4. Even when we doubt whether we have the ability to cheer people up and comfort them, prayer to Jesus our friend becomes a source of strength and confidence to us. The plagues of humanity that we are unable to ward off lose their bite and dread when we place everything in the hands of God, who knows what we can take and does not leave us alone in our predicament. The secret of the

cross of Jesus places all our concerns in the darkness of seeming failure, even our efforts for suffering people, to whom we would want to
impart a blessing. But do we know what people who turn to us in
their hour of loneliness experience internally? We are convinced
that Jesus' experience of being forsaken by God (Matthew 27:46)
nevertheless led to a trusting acceptance of death. Accordingly, we
pray for those who are churned up inwardly and full of doubts. The
insight of a friend probes deeply, cutting through the fog of human
powerlessness. Jesus loves us and does not let us fall, just as he did not
abandon his friend Lazarus and his sisters in the hour of trial. What
he says to Martha, "I am the resurrection and the life," becomes the
source of comfort and of strength. In the resurrected One we, like
Mary Magdalene, recognize Jesus as our Master and loving friend.

Chapter 9
Jesus Our Friend

he highly regarded philosopher of religion and theologian Eugen Biser, successor to the professorship of Karl Rahner in Munich, wrote a book titled "The Friend: Drawing Nearer to Jesus."[1] This publication assumes prior familiarity with two other books: "The Helper" and "Jesus for Christians."[2] The author felt impelled to write this new book about Jesus because times have changed and with them the faith-consciousness of Christians has further developed. We are living in a transitional phase between an institutionally constituted Christianity and one that is mystically internalized. As an attentive observer of the development of beliefs, including the move toward new paradigms and new moods, Eugen Biser has been, like Romano Guardini in his time, an observer of the ever-changing stream of developing ideas, of religious thoughts and tendencies. In this way he puts his finger on the pulse of the time and maintains, along with Karl Rahner, that Christianity will become a mystical religion or else have no future. The point of departure for our understanding of Jesus Christ is not the Christ from above, as the theological fathers describe him, nor the Christ from below, as the modern theologians endeavor to characterize him, but the "Christ from within," who reveals himself to us through our mystical encounter with him. Christendom is now entering its mystical stage, and the best paradigm for that would be the approach to Jesus as friend.

I have certain reservations about the expression "mystical," which has a long history behind it and is used today in various ways. It sounds too mystifying, too mysterious, too esoteric. By contrast, friendship with Jesus recommends itself, because it concerns our external contacts with him as much as our internal relationship. We see Jesus before us as a human being and we feel ourselves inwardly connected to him. He generates the impetus for our actions, especially when it comes to sacrificial service for the poor, sick, and suffering. He calls on us to devote our very life to the friends (John 15:13). Jesus Christ, who offers us his friendship, lived this himself and requires it of us.

Friendship is really a comprehensive expression for our relationship with him. Thereby, as Eugen Biser says, we have distanced ourselves from the lordly manliness of Christ,[3] a notion that Guardini proposed. The friend Jesus calls to us: "Come to me, all you that are weary and are carrying heavy burdens, and I will give you rest. Take my yoke upon you, and learn from me; for I am gentle and humble in heart, and you will find rest for your souls. For my yoke is easy, and my burden is light" (Matthew 11:29–30). That is the voice of the friend who understands us and reveals his heart to us, who makes austere and severe demands upon us, and yet bestows on us rest and joy.

How then can we find comfort amid such inner and outer suffering? The New Testament provides the answer: To be sure, Jesus the Son of God took these afflictions upon himself; he confirmed the way of the cross when, in the hour of extreme darkness, he said to God: "Remove this cup from me; yet, not what I want, but what you want" (Mark 14:36). Looking to the Father (Abba), he endured this hour of trial.

This example of Jesus alone in the Garden is a great encouragement and comfort, because God saved the crucified One and raised him up to new life. This places a familiar thought in a new light, if we see Jesus as our friend who shares with us in the way of suffering and death. I can turn to him in times of need and bitterness and can pray for strength and surrender. He is near to us and leads us through all darkness and desperation. He is a good friend who understands and supports us.

How often have I sensed this among a believing people in covenant with Christ! To be sure, we should also stand with others out of our friendship with Jesus, giving them warmth, love, and friendship in their time of suffering and death. Jesus, my friend, is a help in every situation of life, especially at the point where people have reached the end, knowing no other way of escape.

Notes

Introduction

1. Gerd Lüdemann, *The Resurrection of Jesus: History, Experience, Theology*, trans. John Bowden (Minneapolis: Augsburg Fortress, 1995).

PART ONE:
PORTRAITS OF JESUS

Chapter 1: Picturing Jesus

1. Rudolf Schnackenburg, *Die Person Jesu Christi im Spiegel der vier Evangelien* (Freiburg im Breisgau, 1993; 2d ed. 1994); Engl. trans.: *Jesus in the Gospels: A Biblical Christology*, trans. O. C. Dean, Jr. (Louisville, Ky.: Westminster John Knox Press, 1995).
2. Albert Schweitzer, *The Quest of the Historical Jesus* (1906; 2d ed. 1913; Engl. trans., London, 1910).
3. Page 632 in the German edition (*Geschichte der Leben-Jesu-Forschung*, 6th ed. [Tübingen, 1951]).
4. Werner Georg Kümmel, *Dreissig Jahre Jesusforschung, 1950-1980* (Königstein and Bonn, 1985).

Notes

Chapter 2:
The Revolutionary Jesus

1. Hermann Reimarus, *Von dem Zwecke Jesu und seiner Jünger* (Braunschweig, 1778).
2. Heidelberg, 1929-30.
3. Joel Carmichael, *The Death of Jesus* (New York: Macmillan Co., 1963).
4. S.G.F. Brandon, *Jesus and the Zealots* (New York: Charles Scribner's Sons, 1968).
5. Oscar Cullman, *Jesus and the Revolutionaries*, trans. Gareth Putnam (New York: Harper & Row, 1970).
6. Martin Hengel, *Was Jesus a Revolutionist?* trans. William Klassen (Philadelphia: Fortress Press, 1971).
7. Cf. also Karlheinz Müller's contribution "Möglichkeit und Vollzug jüdischer Kapitalgerichtsbarkeit im Prozess gegen Jesus von Nazareth," in *Der Prozess gegen Jesus: Historische Rückfragen und theologische Deutung*, ed. Karl Kertelge (Freiburg, 1988).
8. Cf. Luise Schottroff and Wolfgang Stegemann, *Jesus of Nazareth, Hope of the Poor*, trans. Matthew J. O'Connell (1978; Maryknoll, N.Y.: Orbis Books, 1986).
9. Karl Kautsky, *Der Ursprung des Christentums: Eine historische Untersuchung* (Stuttgart, 1908).
10. Max Maurenbrecher, *Von Nazareth nach Golgotha* (1909).

Chapter 3:
Jesus of the Essenes

1. K. H. Venturini, *Natürliche Geschichte des grossen Propheten von Nazareth* (1801-1802).
2. J. Lehmann, *Jesus-Report: Protokoll einer Verfälschung* (Düsseldorf, 1970).
3. For example, *Rabbi J: Ein Auseinandersetzung mit Johannes Lehmanns Jesus-Report* (Würzburg, 1970).
4. Michael Baigent and Richard Leigh, *The Dead Sea Scrolls Deception* (New York: Simon & Schuster, 1993).

5. See Klaus Berger, *The Truth under Lock and Key? Jesus and the Dead Sea Scrolls* (Louisville, Ky.: Westminster John Knox Press, 1995).

6. Joseph A. Fitzmyer, *Responses to One Hundred One Questions on the Dead Sea Scrolls* (New York: Paulist Press, 1992).

7. Otto Betz and Reiner Riesner, *Jesus, Qumran, and the Vatican: Clarifications* (New York: Crossroad, 1994).

8. Barbara Thiering, *Jesus and the Riddle of the Dead Sea Scrolls: Unlocking the Secrets of His Life Story* (San Francisco: Harper, 1993).

Chapter 4:
Jesus: Crucified but Not Raised to New Life

1. Gerd Lüdemann, *The Resurrection of Jesus: History, Experience, Theology*, trans. John Bowden (Minneapolis: Augsburg Fortress, 1995).

2. Ibid., 174, citing Erich Fascher, "Die Auferstehung Jesu und ihr Verhältnis zur urchristlichen Verkündigung," *Zeitschrift für die Neutestamentliche Wissenschaft* 26 (1927): 1-26, at p. 5.

3. Regarding the question of visions, cf. H. Kessler, *Sucht den Lebenden nicht bei den Todten!* (Düsseldorf, 1985), 219-36.

4. David Friedrich Strauss, *The Life of Jesus, Critically Examined*, trans. George Eliot (London, 1846).

PART TWO:
JESUS OUR FRIEND—A FASCINATING PORTRAIT

Chapter 5: The Gift of Friendship

1. Aegidius, also known as Giles of Assisi (1190-1262), was a companion of St. Francis of Assisi.

2. Ignatius, *To the Romans*. English translation from William R. Schoedel, *Ignatius of Antioch* (Philadelphia: Fortress Press, 1985), 165.

Notes

Chapter 6:
Friendship according to John and Paul

1. Literally "mouth to mouth," in German and in Greek. English translations typically render the phrase "face to face" [Translator].
2. German: Einsenkung in Gott.

Chapter 7:
Jesus as the Model for Humankind

1. German: Mitmenschlichkeit.
2. Karl Adam, *Christ Our Brother*, trans. Justin McCann (New York: Macmillan Co., 1931).
3. Gerd Theissen, *The Miracle Stories of the Early Christian Tradition*, ed. John Riches, trans. Francis McDonagh (Philadelphia: Fortress Press, 1983).

Chapter 9:
Jesus Our Friend

1. Eugen Biser, *Der Freund: Annäherung an Jesus* (Munich, 1989).
2. Eugen Biser, *Der Helfer* (1973), and *Jesus für Christen* (1984).
3. German: Herrentum Christi. [Cf. Romano Guardini, *The Humanity of Christ: Contributions to a Psychology of Jesus*, trans. Ronald Walls (New York: Pantheon Books, 1964).]